THE

GOLF FANATIC

Other books in the Fanatic series:

The Dog Fanatic

The Cat Fanatic

THE
GOLF
FANATIC

The Best Things Ever Said
by the Pros and Duffers
of the Sport

**Edited and with an Introduction
by Robert McCord**

BOOKS

First published in Great Britain in 2008 by
JR Books, 10 Greenland Street, London NW1 0ND
www.jrbooks.com

Designed by Nancy Freeborn/Freeborn Design

A catalogue record for this book is available from the British Library.

ISBN 978 1 906217 26 6

1 3 5 7 9 10 8 6 4 2

Printed by CPI Bookmarque, Croydon, CR0 4TD

CONTENTS

INTRODUCTION

Golf is almost Shakespearean in its elegant com-
mingling of comedy, absurdity, heroism and tragedy
acted out by a panoply of characters ranging from
weekend duffers, such as myself, to those in the
pantheon of the game, such as Tom Morris, Joyce
Wethered, Bobby Jones, Babe Zaharias, Walter
Hagen, Ben Hogan, Mickey Wright, Arnold Palmer,
Nancy Lopez, Jack Nicklaus and all the rest. Often
golf appears to be a Sisyphean exercise—we always
seem to be pushing a very large boulder up a hill
while venturing along the course. But any anguish
and frustration are alleviated by that occasional
perfect shot, the good company of other golfers,
and the often beautiful and challenging courses
where we match wits with the fates.

The Golf Fanatic is a collection of observations on the game from the great, near great and not too great, who, in their own ways, contribute to its lore and richness. In aggregate, the compiling of these quotes is an attempt to illustrate the richness of the golf experience and its limitless possibilities and limitations—that endless roller coaster we all ride whenever we pick up a club.

I hope that you find some enjoyment among these pages. The pleasure was mine in reading the material to get to this point. But finally I had to stop. Now it's your turn to play.

—Robert McCord
New York City
January 2007

ON
GOLF
DEFINED

Golf: A game probably evolved from Dutch antecedents, first recorded in Scotland in the 15th century, and played under codified rules since the middle of the 18th century; now consisting of hitting a golf ball, using an array of golf clubs, by successive strokes into each of nine or eighteen holes on a golf course.

—FROM THE *RULES OF GOLF*,
PUBLISHED BY THE ROYAL
AND ANCIENT GOLF CLUB IN
ST. ANDREWS, SCOTLAND,
AND THE UNITED STATES
GOLF ASSOCIATION,
FAR HILLS, NEW JERSEY

. . . we saw elderly citizens playing at the Old Scots game of golf, which is a kind of gigantic variety of billiards.

—PETER MORRIS
FROM *PETER'S LETTERS TO HIS KINSFOLK* **(1819)**

No one will ever have golf under his thumb. No round ever will be so good it could not have been better. Perhaps this is why golf is the greatest of games. You are not playing a human adversary; you are playing a game. You are playing old man par.

—BOBBY JONES
THE GREATEST AMATEUR GOLFER OF ALL TIME

Golf is just one thing to me—
the pure pleasure of the
golf swing.

—MICKEY WRIGHT
WINNER OF 82 LPGA
TOURNAMENTS

I think at that time I really fell in love with the game. I'd always loved golf, but now it was a new type of love that I could have.

—TOM WATSON
AFTER HIS ONE-SHOT WIN OVER
JACK NICKLAUS IN THE 1977
BRITISH OPEN

The thing that sets golf apart from the other sports is that it takes self-confidence, an ability to rely totally on yourself. When I'm through, I'll really miss kicking myself to get it done. I can live without playing the Masters. But the really satisfying time is the three weeks leading up to the Masters when I'm preparing for it.

—JACK NICKLAUS
WINNER OF SIX MASTERS (1963, 1965, 1966, 1972, 1975, 1986)

Golf increases the blood pressure, ruins the disposition, spoils the digestion, induces neurasthenia, hurts the eyes, calluses the hands, ties knots in the nervous system, debauches the morals, drives men to drink or homicide, breaks up the family, turns the ductless glands into internal warts, corrodes the pneumogastric nerve, breaks off the edges of the vertebrae, induces spinal meningitis and progressive mendacity, and starts angina pectoris.

—DR. A. S. LAMB
MCGILL UNIVERSITY

The golfer has more enemies than any other athlete. He has fourteen clubs in his bag, all of them different; 18 holes to play, all of them different, every week; and all around him is sand, trees, grass, water, wind and 143 other players. In addition, the game is 50 percent mental, so his biggest enemy is himself.

—DAN JENKINS
GOLF WRITER, DESCRIBING GOLF
ON THE PGA TOUR

Golf is a good walk
spoiled.

—MARK TWAIN

I am a slave to golf.

—ENID WILSON
WINNER OF THE 1925 BRITISH
GIRLS' TITLE

Rock-a-bye, baby—til father comes home;

Father's off golfing and mother's alone;

He phoned me this morning— he wanted his cleek;

Perhaps he'll be home again, sometime next week.

—"MOTHER GOOSE ON THE LINKS," 1909

Golf is about how well you accept, respond to, and score with your misses much more so than it is a game of your perfect shots.

—DR. BOB ROTELLA
**SPORTS PSYCHOLOGIST AND
CONSULTANT TO GOLFERS**

Rail-splitting produced an immortal president in Lincoln, but golf hasn't produced even a good A1 Congressman.

—WILL ROGERS
AMERICAN HUMORIST

Golf courses are the best place to observe ministers, but none of them are above cheating a bit.

—JOHN D. ROCKEFELLER
OIL BILLIONAIRE AND AVID GOLFER

Golf is an awkward set of bodily
contortions designed to produce a
graceful result.

—TOMMY ARMOUR
**GOLF INSTRUCTOR AND WINNER
OF THE U.S. OPEN (1927), PGA
(1930) AND BRITISH OPEN (1931)**

When I was a schoolgirl my idea of good golf was a good drive. What happens afterwards did not matter. I was perfectly content to suffer the most grievous trouble if I smacked the ball 200 yards off the tee. Fortunately, I revised my ideas fairly quickly and settled down to practising the various kinds of approach play, determined to master all of them.

—PAMELA BARTON
WINNER OF BOTH THE BRITISH
LADIES' AND U.S. WOMEN'S
AMATEURS IN 1936

Golf is twenty percent mechanics and technique. The other eighty percent is philosophy, humor, tragedy, romance, melodrama, companionship, camaraderie, cussedness and conversation.

—GRANTLAND RICE

NOTED AMERICAN SPORTS WRITER
AND AVID GOLFER UNTIL HIS
DEATH IN 1954 AT AGE 74

Playing golf is like eating. It's something which has to come naturally.

—SAM SNEAD

WINNER OF A RECORD 81 OFFICIAL PGA TOUR EVENTS

Earl Woods made the most of his mulligan as a parent. He had two boys and a girl in a previous marriage but he regretted he didn't spend enough time with them because of Army demands. He would not make the same mistake the second time around with a son he nicknamed Tiger.

—JEFF RUDE

IN HIS ARTICLE ON EARL WOODS, "THE MAN WHO MOLDED A LEGEND," IN *GOLFWEEK*. EARL WOODS DIED OF CANCER IN APRIL 2006.

I am not talking about ladies' golf because strictly speaking, there is no such thing as ladies' golf—only good or bad golf played by the member of either sex.

—JOYCE WETHERED
WINNER OF FIVE CONSECUTIVE
ENGLISH LADIES' TITLES
(1920-1924) INCLUDING
33 MATCHES IN SUCCESSION

Middle age occurs when you are too young to take up golf and too old to rush up to the net.

—FRANKLIN PIERCE ADAMS

Golf is a game in which you claim the privileges of age and retain the playthings of childhood.

—SAMUEL JOHNSON

I thought everybody was named Labron and Byron, talked with a Texas accent, and said, "Nice shot, padnah."

—AMY ALCOTT

WINNER OF OVER $3 MILLION ON THE LPGA TOUR, ON HOW TELEVISION INFLUENCED HER TO CHOOSE GOLF OVER TENNIS AT AGE 9

I may know I am better than an 18, but the computer absorbs my scores year after year and continues to tell me that is what I am. Therein lies the tragedy of golf. We know what we should be, but there is always some number telling us what it is. . . .

—PETER ANDREWS
GOLF WRITER, ON THE TRAGEDY OF GOLF NUMBERS

Golf is like acting in that both require concentration and relaxation at the same time. In acting, you can't push emotion. You have to let it rise from you naturally. Same thing in golf. You have to have a plan and a focus; but then you need to just let it happen and enjoy the smooth movement of the swing.

—JANE SEYMOUR
ACTRESS AND HIGH HANDICAPPER

Golf is a game in which you try to put a small ball in a small hole with implements singularly unsuited to the purpose.

—WINSTON CHURCHILL

Golf is not, on the whole, a game for realists. By its exactitudes of measurement, it invites the attention of perfectionists.

—HEYWOOD HALE BROUN
AMERICAN SPORTSWRITER

Playing golf is not hot work. Cutting sugar cane for a dollar a day—that's hot work. Hotter than my first wrist watch.

—CHI-CHI RODRIGUEZ

A NATIVE OF BAYAMÓN, PUERTO RICO, AND WINNER OF OVER $6 MILLION ON THE SENIOR PGA TOUR

Every shot in golf should be played as a shot at some clearly defined target. All players realize this when they are playing a shot to the green. A narrow opening between bunkers, or the pin itself, may be the target. But what many of them forget is the shot off the tee should also be aimed at the target down the fairway.

—CRAIG WOOD
WINNER OF THE MASTERS
AND U.S. OPEN IN 1921

The pond'rous club upon the ball
  Descends
Involved in dust th' exulting orb
  Ascends

—THOMAS MATHISON
IN *THE GOFF*, **THE FIRST GOLF**
BOOK EVER WRITTEN, IN 1743

But there is a difference between playing well and hitting the ball well. Hitting the ball well is about thirty percent of it. The rest is being comfortable with the different situations on the course.

—MICKEY WRIGHT

WINNER OF A SINGLE SEASON RECORD 13 LPGA TOUR VICTORIES IN 1963

That's the hard thing, the time it takes to keep yourself prepared. That I still have the discipline and the desire to get out there day after day, beat balls and putt and chip, do my hour of stretching and exercise. I really don't understand why I keep doing that. I guess we could go ask Arnold. I guess it is something that is there in you and never goes away.

—RAYMOND FLOYD
IN A *GOLF DIGEST* INTERVIEW
IN 1994

A round of golf partakes of the journey, and the journey is one of the central myths and signs of Western man . . . if it is a journey, it is also a round: it always leads back to the place where you started from . . . golf is always a trip back to the first tee, the more you play the more you realize you are staying where you are. By playing golf you reenact that secret of the journey. You may even get to enjoy it.

—SHIVAS IRONS

FROM *GOLF IN THE KINGDOM* BY MICHAEL MURPHY (1972)

ON
BEGINNINGS

They say golf came easy to me
because I was a good athlete, but
there's not any girl on the LPGA
Tour who worked near as hard as
I did in golf. It is the toughest
game I ever tackled.

—BABE ZAHARIAS

**WINNER OF 17 CONSECUTIVE
AMATEUR TOURNAMENTS IN 1946
AND 1947 AND A MEMBER OF THE
LPGA HALL OF FAME**

My family was so poor they couldn't afford kids. The lady next door had me.

—LEE TREVINO

The hardest thing was being young and coming onto the tour right out of high school and a very close home environment. I think the thing I missed most was my mother's homemade soup.

—AMY ALCOTT
RECALLING HER EARLY DAYS
ON THE LPGA TOUR

When I was three . . . my father put my hands in his and placed them around the shaft of a cut-down women's golf club. He showed me the classic overlap, or Vardon grip—the proper grip for a good golf swing he said—and told me to hit the golf ball . . . "Hit it hard boy. Go find it and hit it again."

—ARNOLD PALMER
FROM *A GOLFER'S LIFE*, **WITH JAMES DODSON (1999)**

I feel sorry for rich kids now. I really do. Because they're never going to have the opportunity I had. Because I knew tough things, and I had a tough day all my life and can handle tough things. They can't. And every day that I progressed was a joy to me and I recognized it every day. I don't think I could have done it if I hadn't had the tough days to begin with.

—BEN HOGAN
IN *HOGAN* BY CURT SAMPSON
(1998)

The most important advice I'd give any woman just starting to play is: get the fundamentals correct. It's a bad mistake simply to pick up a club and start swinging. If you can afford them, lessons from a competent pro will be worth their weight in birdies; if money is a consideration, join a group to take lessons.

—LOUISE SUGGS
MEMBER OF THE LPGA
HALL OF FAME

If you're going to be a victim of the first few holes, you don't have a prayer. You're like a puppet. You let the first few holes jerk your strings and tell you how you're going to feel and how you're going to think.

—DR. BOB ROTELLA

NOTED SPORTS PSYCHOLOGIST

I had a natural golf swing, they said. With proper instruction, I could hit a golf ball as far, if not farther, than any of the women golfers. Dad was elated. As I came off the course after that round, my destiny was settled. I would become a golfer.

—GLENNA COLLETT
WINNER OF A RECORD SIX
U.S. WOMEN'S AMATEURS,
AFTER PLAYING A FIRST ROUND
OF GOLF WITH HER FATHER

I can only thank Davis Love III
for turning me on to golf and
showing me it isn't a sissy game.

—MICHAEL JORDAN
FORMER NBA SUPERSTAR, WHO
FIRST TOOK UP GOLF IN COLLEGE

Just offer the opportunity. Put the clubs in the corner and give them access to a place to play. That might mean driving them to a course, or just buying them a bicycle. Anything more than that and you can run the risk of turning off your children to a game they could enjoy their whole life. . . .

—NICK PRICE
ON HOW TO BE A GOLFING FATHER

Nobody wants to work for anything. We have a deal for juniors at my club. You caddie, you get free golf. Nobody comes. They'd rather drive their BMWs. You pass baseball fields, nobody is there. They'd rather play Nintendo. When I earned a golf scholarship you had to shoot in the 70s. Now they are giving them to kids who shoot 80.

—JULIE INKSTER
LPGA HALL OF FAMER AND
WINNER OF THREE STRAIGHT
U.S. WOMEN'S AMATEURS
(1980–82)

A kid grows up a lot faster on the golf course; golf teaches you how to behave. You start playing with older people so that a kid who plays golf is different from a lot of athletes in other sports because he hasn't had his own way. He hasn't been spoiled.

—JACK NICKLAUS
**U.S. AMATEUR CHAMPION
IN 1959 AND 1961**

Fight! Fight! Fight! Why is that always preached to a young golfer? After all, if you hold the majority of the good cards, you can stand a fine chance of beating Cuthbertson at bridge. My theory is this: if you perfect your golf shots, your opponent will need more than an unfriendly attitude to defeat you.

—VIRGINIA VAN WIE
A LEADING AMERICAN AMATEUR GOLFER (1934)

There is simply no point at which the notion of pressure becomes intimidating. For Tiger, there cannot be pressure because the worst thing that can happen to him is nothing. His parents still love him and his life will go on as he envisions . . . it is a gift from his parents.

—CHUCK HOGAN
GOLF INSTRUCTOR,
ON TIGER WOODS,
THE YOUNGEST GOLFER TO WIN
THE U.S. AMATEUR CHAMPIONSHIP,
AT AGE 18 IN 1994

Fine. I've frozen enough of my life. Why should you have to?

—BOBO SHEEHAN
TO HIS DAUGHTER, PATTY,
WHEN SHE TOLD HIM, AT AGE 13,
SHE WANTED TO GIVE UP A
PROMISING COMPETITIVE SKIING
CAREER TO PLAY GOLF

I learned by copying. My father used to take Roger and me to watch golf when we were youngsters, and I tried to copy the good players' rhythm. Then, when I began playing fairly well, I played a lot with Roger and his friends from Oxford.

—JOYCE WETHERED
THE WORLD'S LEADING WOMAN
GOLFER IN THE 1920S AND 1930S

Whenever I had gone for several days without seeing her, I would refresh my spirit by repeating to myself: "We don't ever see you playing golf," with the nasal intonation in which she uttered the words, point blank, without moving a muscle in her face. And I thought that there could be no one in the world as desirable.

—MARCEL PROUST
FROM *WITHIN A BUDDING GROVE*

I don't know enough
to take you where you
need to be.

—HARDY LOUDERMILK

**GOLF INSTRUCTOR, TO LPGA HALL
OF FAMER, KATHY WHITWORTH,
WHEN SHE WAS 17**

I needed to be pushed. As a youngster I didn't recognize my true ability or talents. And, yes, I had a little bit of rebellion in me. I wanted to be with the gang. Sure, I said I was going to the golf course, but when I got my driver's license, man, as soon as I got out of sight, I took the next left.

—PAT BRADLEY
WHO WAS INDUCTED INTO THE
LPGA HALL OF FAME IN 1991

Between 10 and 13, you play 54 holes a day with your friends and golf pros give you lessons for free. Then, when you're 16, you go on the Teen Tour. If you make the national boys' team, you travel on your summer vacation playing tournaments. It's very structured, but it isn't like American Little League. It isn't for parents, it's for you.

—JESPER PARNEVIK
DESCRIBING THE DEVELOPMENT OF SWEDISH GOLFERS

Why do I love kids so much? Because I never was a kid myself. I was too poor to be a child, so I never really had a childhood. The biggest present I ever got was a marble.

—CHI-CHI RODRIGUEZ
WHO WON HIS FIRST PGA TOUR
EVENT IN 1963 AT AGE 27

ON
OBSTACLES

Those who the gods
seek to destroy first,
learn how to play golf.

—LESLIE NIELSEN
IN THE VIDEO, *BAD GOLF MY WAY*

The world's No. 1 tennis player spends 90 percent of his time winning, while the world's No. 1 golfer spends 90 percent of his time losing. Golfers are great losers.

—DAVID FEHERTY
JOURNEYMAN PROFESSIONAL

One of the objects in placing hazards is to give the players as much pleasurable excitement as possible.

—ALISTER MACKENZIE
GOLF COURSE ARCHITECT, FROM
HIS CLASSIC *GOLF ARCHITECTURE*

I am among those who firmly believe that a round of golf should not take more than 3½ hours, four at most. Anything longer than that is not a round of golf, it's life in Albania.

—DAN JENKINS
GOLF WRITER, ON SLOW PLAY

Golf was a game supported by rich men who did the hiring and firing, the pros were servants.

—AL BARKOW

**WRITING ABOUT THE LOWLY
STATUS OF PROFESSIONALS
IN THE EARLY DAYS OF GOLF**

Before Hagen broke down the walls of prejudice, a professional golfer had no standing whatever.

—GENE SARAZEN
IN HERBERT WARREN WIND'S,
THE COMPLETE GOLFER (1950)

No dogs or women.

—SIGN AT THE ENTRANCE
TO A GOLF CLUB

The golf links lie so near the mill
    That almost every day
The laboring children can look out
    And watch the men at play.

—SARAH N. CLEGHORN
ON GOLF AND CHILD LABOR IN 1915

How do they learn to play? Courses are so busy and many of them are restrictive for kids. I worry about this.

—BILL OGDEN

FORMER CLUB PROFESSIONAL,
NORTH SHORE COUNTRY CLUB

The only area where I have ever experienced discrimination is athletics. Growing up, I couldn't play little league baseball or be on the high school golf team simply because I was a girl. But that's changing. My alma mater, Furman University, now has five full golf scholarships for women. There weren't any when I went there. . . .

—BETSY KING
WINNER OF THE U.S. WOMEN'S
OPEN IN 1989 AND 1990

Why do men have the right to feel superior? I think women are far superior to men, or at any rate, we're all equal. I don't see why I can't have the same rights as a man.

—MARY ANDERSON
  CHAIR OF THE LADIES' GOLF UNION, REACTING TO DISCRIMINATORY PRACTICES AGAINST LADY GOLFERS IN ENGLAND IN 1991

It's pretty much a miracle that
a bullet can go through your
neck and not hit anything vital.

—**KIM WILLIAMS**
AFTER BEING ACCIDENTALLY SHOT
IN THE NECK BY A STRAY BULLET
FROM A TARGET SHOOTER AT THE
YOUNGSTOWN-WARREN LPGA
CLASSIC IN 1994

Some players would complain if they were playing on Dolly Parton's bedspread.

—JIMMY DEMARET
WINNER OF 31 CAREER
PGA EVENTS

. . . Don't get into the habit of using "winter rules." If you do, you'll never learn to be a decent golfer. "Winter rules" are generally an amusing delusion. They aid neither in the development of the turf nor of the player.

—TOMMY ARMOUR
IN *HOW TO PLAY YOUR BEST GOLF ALL THE TIME* **(1961)**

When facing a hazard, focus your attention sharply on your target, not the hazard.

—DR. BOB ROTELLA
SPORTS PSYCHOLOGIST

When a ball lies on clothes, or within one club length of a washing tub, the clothes may be drawn from under the ball and the tub removed.

—AN 1851 RULE, ISSUED BY THE
   ROYAL & ANCIENT FOR HAZARDS
   CAUSED BY TOWNSWOMEN
   WHO WASHED THEIR CLOTHES IN
   THE SWILCAN BURN, THE WATER
   HAZARD THAT NOW CUTS THE
   FIRST AND EIGHTEENTH FAIRWAYS
   ON THE OLD COURSE

I am a better player than when I was playing really well. Mentally I just don't have the confidence that I had.

—KARRIE WEBB

WHO WON THE 2006 LPGA KRAFT NABISCO MAJOR TOURNAMENT AT RANCHO MIRAGE AFTER A THREE-AND-A-HALF-YEAR MAJOR DROUGHT ON THE LPGA TOUR

Herman, would you check on my clubs?

—BEN HOGAN

TO FELLOW PGA PRO HERMAN KEISER FROM HIS HOSPITAL BED, SHORTLY AFTER HOGAN WAS ALMOST KILLED IN AN AUTOMOBILE ACCIDENT IN 1949

Christ, most people'd be drunk for two days on what I have before dinner.

—JOHN DALY
WINNER OF THE PGA
CHAMPIONSHIP AND BRITISH OPEN.
ON HIS BATTLE WITH ALCOHOLISM

I can't go out and party as much as I want. I have to behave. It's a big change for me and I'm doing it little by little.

—HELEN ALFREDSSON
LPGA TOUR PLAYER

Ma God! It's like playing
up a spout.

—JAMIE ANDERSON
**WINNER OF THREE CONSECUTIVE
BRITISH OPENS (1877–1899),
AFTER HITTING FIVE BALLS OUT
OF BOUNDS ON THE OLD FIRST
HOLE AT HOYLAKE**

The biggest problem we have in golf is course conditions.

—SEVE BALLESTEROS
ON THE POOR CONDITION OF
EUROPEAN TOUR COURSES

I don't like the idea of golf widows. I was raised to believe I could do anything a man can do.

—JANE SEYMOUR
ACTRESS AND 34 HANDICAPPER

I'll be playing center for the Bulls
before Michael plays on the Tour.

—PETER JACOBSEN
**VETERAN PGA TOUR PLAYER,
ASSESSING MICHAEL JORDAN'S
CHANCES OF JOINING THE TOUR**

He's made one of the greatest attempts to play of any athlete I've seen.

—PAYNE STEWART
ON FELLOW PGA PRO
PAUL AZINGER'S FIGHT
AGAINST CANCER IN 1994

I'm so tired of getting operated on.
I'd rather die almost than have another
operation, but I may not have a choice.

—JOHNNY MILLER

**FORMER PGA TOUR PLAYER AND
NBC-TV GOLF COMMENTATOR**

Involving minorities in the game of golf has financial, political and social implications. But the bottom line is simple: the more people who play the game, the fewer problems we'll have in the world. Because the game itself teaches people so much about themselves and others.

—EARL WOODS
FATHER OF ELDRICK "TIGER"
WOODS, WINNER OF THREE
U.S. JUNIOR BOYS AND THREE
U.S. AMATEUR CHAMPIONSHIPS

I don't know if you're ever finished trying to improve. As soon as you feel like you are finished, then I guess you are finished, because you've already put a limit on your ability and what you can attain. I don't think that's right.

—TIGER WOODS
**AFTER WINNING HIS 8TH
TOURNAMENT IN 1999,
THE WORLD GOLF CHAMPIONSHIP
IN SOTOGRANDE, SPAIN**

ON
PRACTICE

Never try a shot you
haven't practiced.

—HARVEY PENICK

**GOLF INSTRUCTOR AND AUTHOR
OF** *HARVEY PENICK'S LITTLE
RED BOOK*

I've never had a coach in my life. When I find one who can beat me, then I'll listen.

—LEE TREVINO

WINNER OF 27 PGA TOUR EVENTS

The more I practice
the luckier I get.

—GARY PLAYER
THIRTEEN-TIME WINNER OF
THE SOUTH AFRICA OPEN

Don't play too much golf if you want to get on in the game. Three rounds a day are too much for any man, and if he makes a practice of playing them whenever he has the opportunity, his game will suffer.

—HARRY VARDON
**WINNER OF A RECORD
SIX BRITISH OPENS**

The strengths of my game were developed in the States. As a student, I found the weather and the facilities were so good that I wanted to practice seven days a week. I put in a helluva lot of effort in college. I wasn't born with this ability. I had to work bloody hard to become the player I am today.

—COLIN MONTGOMERIE
ONE OF EUROPE'S BEST GOLFERS

To score better, you must replicate on-course conditions as much as possible. For example, when practicing putter or bunker play, play one ball until you hole out. By moving around, changing clubs and lies, and playing from wherever the shot ends up, you are forced to make the shots necessary to get up-and-down on the course.

—PIA NILSSON
COACH OF THE SWEDISH
NATIONAL GOLF TEAM,
GOLF MAGAZINE (1997)

I had to learn how to play out
of bunkers because I used to
be in so many of them.

—KEN VENTURI

WINNER OF THE 1964 U.S. OPEN

I'd probably been up to 250, but I just happened to be at 215 at the time. I'd probably be the fat lady in a circus right now if it hadn't been for golf. It kept me on the course and out of the refrigerator.

—KATHY WHITWORTH
**WINNER OF A RECORD
88 LPGA TOUR EVENTS,
ON HER PORTLY YOUTH**

When practising, use the club that gives you the most trouble, and do not waste your time in knocking a ball about with the tool that gives you the most satisfaction and with which you rarely make a bad stroke.

—HARRY VARDON
FROM *THE COMPLETE GOLFER*

It is strange how few bunkers one gets into during pretournament rounds, but in the competition proper they have a habit of almost springing up in the night. So bunker shot practice is very important to test the texture and depth of the sand.

—BILL COX
"SIX POINTERS TO BETTER GOLF" IN
SECRETS OF THE GOLFING GREATS

Once you play in a tournament, you really get hooked on practice.

—BETSY RAWLS

**FOUR-TIME WINNER OF
THE U.S. WOMEN'S OPEN**

Most people want to spend all their time on the golf course, but if they want to be good players they're wasting their time. You've got to hit balls every day.

—LEE TREVINO
WINNER OF THE U.S. OPEN
IN 1968 AND 1971

Don't swing the club, let the club swing you.

—LESLIE NIELSEN
FROM THE VIDEO
BAD GOLF MY WAY

When you're down to four or five balls, put the driver away and try for two good shots with a wedge. Once you've hit your two, pick the other balls up and go home.

—TOM PAXSON
GOLF PROFESSIONAL

They might be able to beat me,
but they can't out-practice me.

—JERRY BARBER
JOURNEYMAN PGA TOUR
PROFESSIONAL

Practice is not to take the place of teaching, but to make teaching worthwhile.

—HARVEY PENICK

INSTRUCTOR TO TOM KITE, BEN CRENSHAW AND OTHER STARS

I was all right teaching kids and beginners because they will listen. It's the 15-handicappers with bad grips who won't. Maybe if I charged them $500 an hour they would, but I couldn't so I told them to bugger off.

—SIMON HOBDAY
PGA SENIOR TOUR PLAYER,
EXPLAINING WHY HE STOPPED
BEING A CLUB PROFESSIONAL
IN THE 1980S

First thing you have to do is get a room with blackout curtains. Start with full wedge shots. The window won't break. You can pretty much go through your short irons and not break the window.

—ANDREW MAGEE
PGA TOUR PLAYER,
ON PRACTICING IN MOTEL ROOMS

Golf is a constant battle against par, and if you play it any other way, you are encouraging sloppy thinking and sloppy strokes. Ignore the social or business engagement on the golf course, therefore, and play medal whenever possible.

—GARY PLAYER
IN *SECRETS OF*
THE GOLFING GREATS

I don't know why you're practicing so hard to finish second.

—BABE ZAHARIAS

TO LPGA PLAYERS PRACTICING BEFORE A TOURNAMENT

Dig it out of the ground
like I did.

—BEN HOGAN

**IN RESPONSE TO A REQUEST
FOR INSTRUCTION**

All golfers at some time or another get
to the stage where they feel that they
have reached the limit of their capabilities
and that they cannot improve any further.
. . . There is no way of telling yourself
that this kind of streak will come to an
end, it's just a matter of perseverance.

—GEORGE WILL
IN *GOOD ADVICE FOR MEN AND
WOMEN GOLFERS*

Stick your butt out

Mr. President.

—SAM SNEAD'S ADVICE TO
PRESIDENT EISENHOWER,
WHEN IKE ASKED WHY
HIS SWING WAS RESTRICTED

Thank God!
Now, I'll never have
to practice again.

—DOROTHY GERMAIN PORTER
**IN 1977 AFTER WINNING THE U.S.
SENIOR WOMEN'S AMATEUR**

ON
EQUIPMENT

FAR AND SURE.

—MOTTO ON WILLIE PARK'S COAT,
MUSSELBURGH RED
WITH BLUE COLLAR

The finale in freak putters has apparently not yet come, for after nearly every shape of iron, wood and aluminum had been exhausted in an effort to give golfers an implement that would hole a ball regardless of the player's skill, a Chicago professional has come to the front with a putter made of gaspipe.

—*NEW YORK TIMES* ARTICLE,
JULY 27, 1922

In order to preserve the balance between power and the length of holes and in order to retain the special features of the game, the power of the ball should be limited.

—THE ROYAL & ANCIENT RULES OF GOLF COMMITTEE RECOMMENDATION IN 1919

The most important item was the plus fours, a kind of knickers that had to hang exactly right if they were to make the wearer look like Gene Sarazen or Walter Hagen, not like a guy who put on his mother's bloomers by mistake.

—RICHARD ARMOUR
IN HIS BOOK *GOLF IS A FOUR-LETTER WORD* (1962)

I had a fifteenth club in my bag
this week. It was Harvey Penick.

—BEN CRENSHAW
WHO WON THE 1995 MASTERS
AFTER SERVING AS PALLBEARER
FOR HIS MENTOR, HARVEY PENICK

I had been a test pilot for Foot Joys forever. I test their sixty-five-dollar alligator models to see if standing in them for long periods of time in a bar brings any serious harm. What effect spilling beer has on them.

—GEORGE LOW
**EXPERT PUTTER AND
GOLF HUSTLER**

Nice clods Stadler.
Did you get those at a
Buster Brown fire sale?

—FUZZY ZOELLER
KIDDING CRAIG STADLER
ABOUT HIS SHOES

Look at those spoiled bastards.
They don't know the value of a dollar.

—GENE SARAZEN
COMMENTING ON TOURING PROS
WHO DROPPED NEW BALLS
RATHER THAN SEARCH FOR SHOTS
HIT IN THE ROUGH

Why do I wear a red sport shirt on Sundays? Well, if I play bad on the last round of a tournament and cut my throat, it blends.

—LEE TREVINO
EARLY IN HIS PROFESSIONAL CAREER

The lofted club is the answer. It is difficult to control a ball with a straight-faced club. Only a few players can do it. The straight-faced club gains distance but it loses accuracy. . . .

—CRAIG WOOD
ON WHY HE DIDN'T USE A DRIVER
OFF THE TEE

Always use the club that takes the least out of you. Play with a long iron instead of forcing your shot with a short iron. Never say, "Oh, I think I can reach it with such and such a club." There ought never to be any question of your reaching it, so use the next more powerful club in order that you will have a little in hand.

—HARRY VARDON
WINNER OF THE U.S. OPEN IN 1900

Clubs meant nothing to Rolland. He had two or three of them tied round with a bit of string.

—RALPH SMITH
COMMENTING ON DOUGLAS ROLLAND, BIG HITTER AMONG LATE 19TH CENTURY BRITISH GOLF PROFESSIONALS

No one would ever believe that any man ever played with that club in an international match.

—JOHN WARD

FORMER MAJOR LEAGUE
BASEBALL PLAYER AND 1922
WALKER CUP UMPIRE,
COMMENTING ON BERNARD
DARWIN'S SPOON-LIKE BRASSIE
AT THAT FIRST WALKER CUP
CONTEST

You better use a putter cover, because you can put a dent in the face just by breathing on it.

—BOBBY GRACE
GOLF CLUB DESIGNER,
DISCUSSING HIS "FAT LADY
SWINGS" SOFT-FACED PUTTER

With wooden shafts you could stay on the ball longer. The club face stayed with the ball longer—that is, the ball did not leave it so quickly. You retained the feel longer. The ball didn't spring away from you.

—JOYCE WETHERED
DESCRIBED BY BOBBY JONES
AS THE BEST GOLFER HE
HAD EVER SEEN, EXPLAINING
THE DIFFERENCE BETWEEN
STEEL-SHAFTED AND HICKORY-
SHAFTED CLUBS

I'm sure this looks like I'm all over the charts, but it's what works out best for me. I test each club to find my personal preference, so there's a little bit of trial and error involved.

—LOREN ROBERTS
1994 U.S. OPEN RUNNER-UP,
ON WHY HE CARRIES CLUBS
FROM SEVERAL MANUFACTURERS
IN HIS BAG

The gutta-percha ball made all the difference to golf because the game would have dried out if a cheaper ball hadn't come in. The feather ball cost three to five shillings, which made it more expensive than the club. A man could only make three of them a day. . . .

—BOBBY BURNET
CLUB LIBRARIAN OF THE ROYAL &
ANCIENT ON GOLF TECHNOLOGY

You begin to get the idea that maybe golf manufacturers are out of control when you find out they are making clubs and balls out of components used in nuclear weapons and bullet-proof vests.

—E. M. SWIFT
**SPORTS WRITER,
ON MODERN-DAY EQUIPMENT**

We're in America aren't we? If people want to buy a Chevy or Cadillac, they should be able to buy one. If you can build a better golf club, you should build it. When a lot of us are having trouble hitting the ball 220, or 120 yards, why should we be punished because Greg Norman can hit it 320 yards?

—**KARSTEN SOLHEIM**
FOUNDER OF PING AND OPPONENT
OF SOME USGA RESTRICTIONS ON
EQUIPMENT DESIGN

ON THE
MENTAL
GAME

I was young and righteous, but you cannot become a champion without the ability to cope with your emotions. That is the most important factor in becoming a winner. This is what it's all about—being able to control every emotion: elation, dejection, fear, greed, the whole lot.

—MICKEY WRIGHT
**WINNER OF THE 1952
U.S. GIRLS' JUNIOR**

You seem to forget that luck is a part of the game and a good golfer must be good at all parts of the game.

—WALTER TRAVIS
THREE-TIME WINNER OF THE U.S.
AMATEUR (1900–01, 1903), WHEN IT
WAS SUGGESTED TO HIM THAT HE
LOST THE U.S. AMATEUR BECAUSE
OF AN OPPONENT'S LUCK

Train yourself to accept the fact that as a human being you are prone to mistakes. Take pride in being emotionally resilient and mentally tough.

—DR. BOB ROTELLA
SPORTS PSYCHOLOGIST

I don't even know if there was a Mulligan. But he gave his name to a wonderful gesture—letting you play a bad first drive over, and no penalty.

—REX LARDNER
WRITER, IN HIS BOOK *OUT OF THE BUNKER AND INTO THE TREES*

From a quiet house or a secluded part of a hotel, she would come to the first tee, smile charmingly at her opponent when they met at the commencement of their game, and then, almost as though in a trance, become a golfing machine. . . . This cloak of inhumanity was not created to frighten the enemy; it served to conceal an intense concentration, and to conserve its owner's physical strength.

—ENID WILSON
GOLF JOURNALIST,
ON JOYCE WETHERED

To play well you must feel tranquil and at peace. I have never been troubled by nerves in golf because I felt I had nothing to lose and everything to gain.

—HARRY VARDON
**MEMBER OF
THE GOLF HALL OF FAME**

Of all the hazards,
fear is the worst.

—SAM SNEAD

The only problem in major golf is, as ever "how to score," for nearly all the players setting out on the circuits can hit the ball. That is no problem. It is the scoring which counts. I think that to score in golf is a matter of confidence, if you think you cannot do it, then there is no chance that you will.

—HENRY COTTON

The point is that it doesn't matter if you look like a beast before or after the hit, as long as you look like a beauty at the moment of impact.

—SEVE BALLESTEROS
WINNER OF TWO MASTERS
(1980, 1983) AND
THREE BRITISH OPENS
(1979, 1984. 1988)

Concentration is not an element that should be applied all the way around a golf course. It is not the least bit important until you are ready to shoot. There's plenty of time to concentrate when you step up to the ball.

—JULIUS BOROS
IN HIS BOOK
HOW TO PLAY PAR GOLF

It [championships] is something like a cage. First you are expected to get into it and then you are expected to stay there. But of course, nobody can stay there. Out you go—and then you are trying your hardest to get back in again. Rather silly isn't it, when golf—just golf—is so much fun?

—BOBBY JONES
EXPLAINING WHY HE RETIRED
FROM MAJOR COMPETITIVE GOLF
IN 1930 AT AGE 28

The bored haughty face that she turned to the world concealed something—most affectations concealed something eventually, even though they don't in the beginning—and one day I found out what it was. . . . At her first big golf tournament there was a row that nearly reached the newspapers—a suggestion that she had moved her ball from a bad lie in the semi-final round.

—F. SCOTT FITZGERALD
IN *THE GREAT GATSBY* (1925)

Every game of golf that has ever been played—whether the medal was 68 of 168—has taken place on a golf course that measured eight inches or less. I arrived at the dimensions of this golf course by taking a ruler and measuring my own head from back to front.

—EDDIE LOOS

AMERICAN GOLF PROFESSIONAL AND TEACHER

It was kind of a process of self-isolation, of going into a shell, of putting away outside things. Crack American women golfers are adept at it. They brought it to the point of perfection. They never talk . . . they seem to press a button and all at once, in their own minds, nobody else exists.

—PAM BARTON

BRITISH GOLFER, PREPARING FOR THE 1936 U.S. WOMEN'S AMATEUR

The greedy golfer will go too
near and be sucked into his
own destruction.

—JOHN L. LOW
SCOTTISH AMATEUR GOLFER,
GOLF WRITER AND ARCHITECT

Perhaps the best explanation is that Mac was harried in these events by some psychic injury sustained in his first mishaps that, fed by his subsequent failure to produce in the Opens, grew into a complex of such obstinate proportions that the harder he fought to defeat it, the more viciously it defeated him.

—HERBERT WARREN WIND
**WRITER, ON WHY
MACDONALD SMITH COULDN'T
WIN THE BIG ONES**

If profanity had an influence on the flight of the ball, the game of golf would be played far better than it is.

—HORACE G. HUTCHINSON
**BRITISH GOLFER AND
PIONEER GOLF WRITER**

It got worse and worse. It got to where I just hated to go out to the golf course because I knew I couldn't play anymore. There was panic and fear because I didn't know where the ball was going or whether I'd even hit it! To actually fear playing golf after having done so well is a terrible experience.

—KATHY WHITWORTH

WINNER OF 88 LPGA EVENTS,
DESCRIBING WHAT IT WAS LIKE
TO BE IN A SLUMP

The average golfer, I can say flatly, lacks the ability to concentrate, which probably is the most important component of any good game. I believe the ability to concentrate is the difference in skill between the club player and the golf professional, even more than the shot-making process.

—DOW FINSTERWALD

Jack Nicklaus, when one of the brightest amateur stars, won a major championship without using anything longer than a six-iron for his second shots on par-four holes and was home in two on the majority of par fives with an iron. Nicklaus not only enjoys a tremendous advantage percentage-wise but also holds a substantial psychological edge over his opponents with his long ball.

—ARNOLD PALMER
IN *ARNOLD PALMER'S GOLF BOOK*

I find a better way to let it go. I do something physical to feel better, like slam the club in the rough, slam my bag, or slap a tree.

—TOM LEHMAN
PGA PROFESSIONAL

When I left the course after a round this year, a lady told me my biorhythms were off. I told her my golf game was off.

—JACK NICKLAUS
WINNER OF AT LEAST ONE PGA
TOURNAMENT FOR SEVENTEEN
CONSECUTIVE YEARS (1962-78),
IN 1978

When we first arrived, some of the players were talking about how nervous they were. I squelched that right away. I want no negativity. I wanted everything and everybody up. I told them if they were nervous I would get them some Vaseline for their teeth to quiet the chattering noise.

—JOANNE CARNER
CAPTAIN OF THE VICTORIOUS
1994 U.S. SOLHEIM CUP TEAM

Instead of putting pressure on myself and thinking, "I've got to make this shot," I just thought, "Go ahead and make it." It's a subtle difference but a big one.

—COREY PAVIN

AFTER SINKING A 141-YARD, 9-IRON
SHOT AT A CRITICAL POINT
IN THE 1993 RYDER CUP

And finally, he won by being Tiger Woods again. Trying to heal after the loss of his father will be a continual evolution, but clearly he was more focused and game-ready at Hoylake than he'd been at Winged Foot a month ago.

—JEFF BABINEAU

IN HIS ARTICLE "TIGER RESTORES ROAR" IN *GOLFWEEK* AFTER TIGER WOODS WON THE BRITISH OPEN AT ROYAL LIVERPOOL BY TWO STROKES AND HIS ELEVENTH MAJOR PROFESSIONAL TOUR WIN, LEAVING HIM SEVEN MAJORS BEHIND JACK NICKLAUS, THE ALL-TIME LEADER, AT AGE 31

You go out and play your game. Sometimes it comes out as 68 and sometimes at 74. That's not fatalism, that's golf.

—PETER OOSTERHUIS

AFTER BEING CRITICIZED AS "FATALISTIC" RATHER THAN ASSERTIVE ON THE PROFESSIONAL TOUR

Imagine what it was like for me. One day it's John Philip Sousa marches and razor sharp creases in my whites. I'm the All-American boy, blond and bright. The next day I'm in a padded cell in a straitjacket. They gave me a series of six shock treatments in three months.

—BERT YANCEY

FORMER PGA TOUR PLAYER, DESCRIBING THE START OF HIS MANIC DEPRESSION WHILE A WEST POINT CADET IN 1960

I love to watch "Oprah," "Geraldo," all the shows about dysfunctionals. That's my psychoanalysis. I realized I wasn't as bad as I thought.

—MAC O'GRADY
PGA TOUR PROFESSIONAL

I feel my composure is a hundred percent better now than, say, a year ago. I think our galleries enjoy seeing some emotion from the players. I don't think there's anything wrong with showing your temper as long as you don't damage the course or do something to disturb another player. Too many of our players are like robots.

—BETH DANIEL
IN 1980, HER SECOND YEAR ON THE
LPGA TOUR, COMMENTING AFTER
BEING FINED FOR CLUB-THROWING

When Se Ri Pak saw Karrie Webb for the first time following Webb's playoff victory at the Kraft Nabisco Championship, Pak could not wait to give her friend a congratulatory embrace. Pak and Webb had struggled through similar issues the previous twenty-four months and Pak was there to show her support. After a five-minute chat, Pak left with one final comment. She said, "Good to see you back playing well, now it's my turn. I will win the next one," Webb recalled.

—SE RI PAK WON THE MCDONALD'S LPGA IN 2006

I motivate myself by thinking of my family. If I can't be with them at home, I'd rather make my time out here worthwhile. If I play well, I feel like I can justify being away from them—it's okay to leave them that week. If I don't play well, then I feel like I've wasted time I could have spent with them.

—NANCY LOPEZ
LPGA HALL OF FAMER
AND MOTHER OF THREE

I was so nervous today I was almost jumping out of my skin all day. Usually when I'm playing decent, I'm nervous.

—TOM WATSON
ON WINNING THE 1981 MASTERS

We have to be pretty self-centered and confident in ourselves to be successful on the Tour. We have strong personalities—maybe even more so than other professions—because we have to depend solely on our own abilities. My faith has tempered that self-centered streak and helped me to look beyond my own needs to the needs of others.

—BETSY KING
IN 1994, AFTER BECOMING
A CHRISTIAN GOLFER

That way you can understand why you're driving yourself crazy.

—ALLISON FINNEY

LPGA PROFESSIONAL,
EXPLAINING WHY
SHE MAJORED IN PSYCHOLOGY

We've lost our national way. We are a society of Chip Becks laying up intelligently.

—TOM CALLAHAN

WRITER, COMMENTING ON MODERN AMERICAN GOLF IN 1995

Golf is in the interest of good health and good manners. It promotes self-interest and affords a chance to play the man and act the gentleman.

—WILLIAM HOWARD TAFT
THE FIRST U.S. PRESIDENT
TO PLAY SERIOUS GOLF

ON
SWINGS

A golf swing is a collection
of corrected mistakes.

—CAROL MANN

WINNER OF 38 LPGA EVENTS

Long swing, long career.
Short swing, short career.

—JACK BURKE, JR.
MEMBER OF THE PGA
HALL OF FAME

His wriggling at the address has been likened to a man squirming his way into a telephone box with a load of parcels in his arms.

—RALPH GULDAHL'S SWING
DESCRIBED IN *THE ENCYCLOPEDIA OF GOLF* (1975)

It comes and it goes. It's the kind of thing you can't turn loose once you've got it going or it might never come back.

—CRAIG WOOD

COMMENTING ON THE ELUSIVENESS OF A GROOVED GOLF SWING PRIOR TO THE 1941 U.S. OPEN

The golfing public has, in the last few decades, been steered away from golf as a game of feel. The emphasis today is on the mechanics of the swing. As you may have already noticed, I think this is the wrong path.

—JIM FLICK
**NOTED GOLF INSTRUCTOR, IN A
1997** *GOLF MAGAZINE* **ARTICLE**

He didn't know enough about the swing to come back.

—GEORGE FAZIO
ON RALPH GULDAHL'S INABILITY
TO CHANGE FROM BEING AN
INSTINCTUAL GOLFER WHO
COULDN'T CORRECT HIS MISTAKES

If ah didn't have these ah'd hit it twenty yards farther.

—BABE ZAHARIAS

DESCRIBING HOW HER BREASTS IMPEDED HER GOLF SWING

JoAnne has a swing like Babe (Zaharias) did. JoAnne has the power that Babe had and the same sort of three-quarter swing. She also had the Babe's communication with her galleries.

—MARILYN SMITH
ON JOANNE GUNDERSON
CARNER'S SWING

. . . a fidgety player who addressed the ball as if he could reason with it.

—A CHARACTERIZATION OF
  PRESIDENT WOODROW WILSON'S
  GOLF GAME

. . . even God can't hit a 1-iron.

—LEE TREVINO
SUGGESTING THAT HOLDING
A 1-IRON ALOFT MIGHT PROTECT
A GOLFER FROM LIGHTNING IN
A THUNDERSTORM

At this meeting, it was possible for the serious-minded to make a comparison between the English and Scottish swings, and the opinion was the Scottish swings were quicker and shorter.

—FROM THE MINUTES OF A MEETING
OF THE FIRST LADIES' GOLF UNION
IN 1895

The golfer's left side must be the dominant part of the swing. This is the only way to get maximum power and accuracy. If the right side takes over, there is no golf swing.

—KATHY WHITWORTH
LPGA HALL OF FAMER

. . . a physicist can describe the perfect golf swing and write it down in scientific language, but the smart golfer doesn't read it. The smart golfer gives it to his opponent to contemplate.

—DR. FRAN PIROZOLLO
SPORTS PSYCHOLOGIST

I sometimes lose control of my emotions so completely, that I don't know where I am or that it's me hitting the ball.

—MICKEY WRIGHT
WINNER OF 82 TOURNAMENTS
ON THE LPGA TOUR,
DURING HER EARLY YEARS

The shank—of all the golfing diseases, shanking is by far the most outrageous in its devastating results.

—ROGER WETHERED
FROM *THE GAME OF GOLF* **(1931)**

I found that seeing the swinge of your body by turning it upon your legge is the largest and strongest motion. Therefor it must begin first and the turning at the small of the back must only second it, and then must follow the motion at the shoulders.

—THOMAS KINCAID
FROM HIS DIARY IN *THE BOOK OF THE OLD EDINBURGH CLUB* **(1687)**

What I mean is, that you must not begin
the downward swing as if you were
anxious to get it over. Haste spells
disaster and disaster is disheartening.
I am always on the look-out against
a pupil becoming downhearted.

—ALEXANDER "SANDY" HERD
BRITISH GOLFER AND INSTRUCTOR

I don't like mechanics. The best swing is the one with the least mechanics. When you see George Duncan or Harry Vardon or Bobby Jones swing, do you notice any mechanics? I don't want my pupils to bother their heads about mechanics, or which hand takes the club up, and which sends it down.

—STEWART MAIDEN
GOLF PROFESSIONAL AND
INSTRUCTOR OF BOBBY JONES,
ALEXA STIRLING AND OTHERS

Readers are reminded that the word "yip" was invented by T. D. Armour the great teacher of golf . . . Armour defines "yips" as a "brain spasm which impairs the short game." "Impairs" is a euphemism.

—STEPHEN POTTER
IN HIS BOOK
GOLFSMANSHIP (1968)

Don't you wish you could hit the ball like that?

—BABE ZAHARIAS

WINNER OF 31 LPGA EVENTS, DEMONSTRATING HOW TO DRIVE AT A GOLF CLINIC

Long driving is of prime importance in golf. It need not be long enough to give the golfer some chance against par, and to put him on good terms with himself.

—TED RAY
**WINNER OF THE BRITISH OPEN
(1912) AND THE U.S. OPEN (1920)**

Bob Hope's swing? I've seen better swings on a condemned playground.

—BING CROSBY
SINGER AND FOUNDER OF
THE PGA BING CROSBY PRO-AM

I may go for it or I may not. It all depends on what I elect to do on my backswing.

—BILLY JOE PATTON
IN THE 1954 MASTERS

Jones: Mr. Vardon, did you ever see a worse shot than that?

Vardon: No.

—HARRY VARDON'S REPLY TO
BOBBY JONES WHEN HE SKULLED
A NIBLICK IN THE 1920 U.S. OPEN

Never saw one who was
worth a damn.

—HARRY VARDON

**1900, COMMENTING ON
LEFT-HANDED GOLFERS**

Harry Vardon was a big man with huge hands. My own was practically lost in his hand shake. He was reserved, quiet, with almost nothing to say. But I learned plenty from watching him swing a golf club. He had a much more compact and precise swing than I had ever seen. He had it in a groove and I tried it out in practice and it worked for me too.

—WALTER HAGEN
OBSERVING HARRY VARDON
AT THE 1913 U.S. OPEN
AT THE COUNTRY CLUB

If your swing was good enough to win one out there, it's good enough to win again. Your problem isn't usually your swing. It's your heart.

—MARK MCCUMBER
WINNER OF OVER $4 MILLION
ON THE PGA TOUR

I didn't want to (shoot for the pin) but there's this thing in my brain that just shoved the ball over there.

—FRED COUPLES
EXPLAINING HOW HE ALMOST HIT
A TEE SHOT INTO RAE'S CREEK
ON THE 12TH HOLE IN THE FINAL
ROUND OF HIS 1992 MASTERS WIN

Flat-footed golf, sir, flat-footed golf.

—J. H. TAYLOR

**WINNER OF FIVE BRITISH OPENS,
DESCRIBING HIS GOLF TECHNIQUE**

A mis-hit. She caught it and it just rolled and rolled.

—MIC POTTER

FURMAN UNIVERSITY COACH,
COMMENTING ON ALL-AMERICAN
CAROLINE PEEK'S WINNING
278-YARD SMASH IN
THE 1992 NCAA CHAMPIONSHIP
LONG DRIVE CONTEST

If you must, let your practice swing be the one where you think of mechanics. Once your mechanics feel right, take a trial swing to concentrate on the target and the feel.

—DR. BOB ROTELLA
SPORTS PSYCHOLOGIST

In using the word rhythm I am not speaking of the swing. The rhythm I have reference to here could also be described as the order of procedure. Walter Hagen was probably the greatest exponent of the kind of rhythm I have in mind to play golf.

—BEN HOGAN
IN HIS BOOK *POWER GOLF* (1948)

The golf swing is a knack requiring the unself-consciousness and the confidence with which people bicycle or swim. Such skills are only acquired by associating certain movements with particular effects, and only after innumerable falls and swallowing a considerable amount of water.

—ENID WILSON
BRITISH GOLFER AND JOURNALIST

It was a very lonely life. But making a change in a golf swing takes a long time, and winter is time for making changes. You do it over and over again, and it is so long before you can see the change that you sometimes wonder why you are doing it at all.

—SANDRA PALMER
**IN "SANDRA PALMER: SHE CAN HANDLE THE PRESSURE"
BY SARAH BALLARD IN**
SPORTS ILLUSTRATED **(1975)**

I accept the fact that I'm going to miss it sometimes. I just hope I miss it where I can find it.

—FUZZY ZOELLER
**WINNER OF THE 1979 MASTERS
AND THE 1984 U.S. OPEN**

I just vomit when I hear 'em talk about the bump-and-run because you just can't do it here.

—PETE DYE

GOLF COURSE DESIGNER, COMMENTING ON HOW THE BUMP-AND-RUN SHOT HAS BEEN ELIMINATED BY HEAVILY WATERED FAIRWAYS ON U.S. GOLF COURSES

. . . he [I] just happened to be hitting just the right sort of ball for the day.

—JOHN BALL
EIGHT-TIME WINNER OF THE
BRITISH AMATEUR, EXPLAINING
HOW HE WON A MEDAL
COMPETITION IN THE WIND
AT HOYLAKE

Some years ago, quite a little publicity was given to the fact that Miss Helen Hicks used wood clubs with the word "oompah" stamped on the head. She explained that she allowed this word, with the first syllable dwelt upon, to run through her mind as she was getting ready to play a stroke to improve her sense of timing.

—BOBBY JONES
COMMENTING ON THE TECHNIQUE OF HELEN HICKS

I have a hook. It nauseated me. I could vomit when I see one. It's like a rattlesnake in your pocket.

—BEN HOGAN
WINNER OF 9 MAJOR GOLF TOURNAMENTS

Two balls in the water. By God, I've got a good mind to jump in and make it four.

—SIMON HOBDAY
WINNER OF THE 1994 U.S.G.A.
SENIOR CHAMPIONSHIP

I shot scenes fast and unworried, much like Julius Boros shoots golf: Walk up to the ball, hit it, laugh, and walk on without losing a stride.

—FRANK CAPRA

FILM DIRECTOR, DESCRIBING
HOW HE MADE THE ACADEMY
AWARD-WINNING FILM
IT HAPPENED ONE NIGHT

Pavin's swing must be the swing of the future, because I sure as hell haven't seen anything like it in the past.

—CHARLES PRICE

GOLF WRITER, COMMENTING ON A SLUMPING COREY PAVIN IN THE 1980S

. . . present day golfers have chopped down their swing action to the barest essentials—go back and come down. This simplification occurred because modern equipment—tailored heads, steel shafts, firmer gripping, better distribution of weight and torque—permits the development of more power with less effort . . .

—DOUG FORD
PGA TOUR PROFESSIONAL

Grip it and rip it.

—JOHN DALY

**WINNER OF THE 1991
PGA CHAMPIONSHIP**

ON
PUTTING

I swear that ball saw more lip than Bianca Jagger on her wedding night. But the kiss never came.

—PETER JACOBSEN
PGA TOUR JOURNEYMAN,
LAMENTING A MISSED PUTT

Hell, I'd putt sitting up
in a coffin if I thought I
could hole something.

—GARDNER DICKINSON
**JUSTIFYING HIS STRANGE
PUTTING STANCE**

Schenectady: A center-shafted putter with an aluminum head, patented by Arthur F. Knight of Schenectady, New York in 1903, used by Walter J. Travis in winning the British Amateur Championship in 1904, and shortly thereafter banned by the Royal & Ancient.

—PETER DAVIES
FROM *THE HISTORICAL DICTIONARY OF GOLF* **(1992)**

To such a perfect putter as Mr. Travis, who would putt if need were with an umbrella or walking-stick, doubtless there are no difficulties.

—ARTHUR POLTOW
IN THE *ILLUSTRATED OUTDOOR NEWS* **(1906)**

Putting is always the great equaliser, because if you are putting well then it takes a lot of pressure off the rest of your game. You can afford to make a few mistakes if you're holing ten- and fifteen-footers for par.

—TOM WATSON
IN 1999, REMEMBERING WHEN HE
WON THE 1975 BRITISH OPEN AT
CARNOUSTIE

The devoted golfer is an anguished soul who has learned a lot about putting just as an avalanche victim has learned a lot about snow.

—DAN JENKINS
NOTED AMERICAN GOLF WRITER

To many, Bolt's putter has spent more time in the air than Lindbergh.

—JIMMY DEMARET
COMMENTING ON THE CLUB-THROWING HABITS OF TOMMY BOLT

On the putting green the mind
can be a grave source of trouble.
Begin to dislike the look of a
putt, and the chances of holing
it at once become less.

—JOYCE WETHERED
FOUR-TIME WINNER OF THE
BRITISH LADIES' CHAMPIONSHIP
(1922, 1924–25, 1929)

When hitting an approach putt, try to lay the ball into an imaginary three-foot circle around the hole. I feel a definite hit with my right hand on both long and short putts. I recommend a rather long and unhurried backswing in putting because it makes the stroke smoother and eliminates the putting yips which sometimes besets golfers who have short, compact backswings.

—BILLY CASPER
MEMBER OF THE PGA
HALL OF FAME

Forget the idea of a three-foot target area around the hole on long putts. Archers and pistol shooters aim for bulls-eyes, not the outer circles. Aim to make the putt.

—DR. BOB ROTELLA
SPORTS PSYCHOLOGIST

Fact one: anyone with normal coordination can become the best putter in the world. Fact two: great putting can make up for many other faults during a round. But no one putts well day-in and day-out if they don't first believe they are a great putter.

—PIA NILSSON
**COACH OF THE SWEDISH
NATIONAL GOLF TEAM**

The more you miss, the worse it gets. The worse it gets, the more likely you are to miss again.

—DAVE PELZ WITH JAMES A. FRANK
FROM THE ARTICLE "YOU NEED A RITUAL," *GOLF MAGAZINE* (1997)

I think I have a real good stroke, I really do, but I swear, I'm the queen of the lip-out and the rim-out. The ball comes out and looks up at me and grins, as if to say "too bad, you missed again." I just don't know how to die the ball into the cup.

—PAT BRADLEY
WINNER OF 31 LPGA, IN 1979,
AT THE AGE OF 28

That shot cost me the championship.

—JOCK HUTCHINSON'S

**COMMENT ON HIS MISSED THREE-
FOOT PUTT FOR BIRDIE ON THE
69TH HOLE AT INVERNESS IN THE
1920 U.S. OPEN**

If I could just putt. I might just
scare somebody, maybe me.

—JACK NICKLAUS
AFTER TWO ROUNDS OF
THE 1986 MASTERS, WHICH
HE WON A RECORD SIXTH TIME

I made that putt. It just didn't go in.

—TOM KITE

**EXPLAINING HIS MISSED 12-FOOTER
ON THE 72ND HOLE TO LOSE BY
ONE STROKE IN THE 1986 MASTERS**

I had never seen or heard of a bent grass green before. I had played on sand greens and Bermuda, but these were frightening, slick and fast. I three-putted everything.

—BYRON NELSON

REMEMBERING HIS FIRST EXPERIENCE WITH BENT GRASS GREENS IN THE 1934 U.S. AMATEUR

Q: Thirteen? How the hell did you make 13 on a par-5?

Arnold Palmer: Missed a 12-footer for 12.

—ARNOLD PALMER
EXPLAINING HOW HE MADE A 12 IN
THE 1961 LOS ANGELES OPEN

I putt so bad I'm gonna
eat a can of Alpo.

—LEE TREVINO
DURING A TOURNAMENT IN 1975

Put me on a putting green in Miami
for a week and I'll kill more tourists than
the Fountainbleau.

—GEORGE LOW
PUTTING HUSTLER

There are many ways to punish a putter, such as burning, rusting and drowning, but the most tortuous is to drag it along pavement out of the door of a fast-moving vehicle.

—DAN JENKINS
PRESENTING ONE OF HIS TEN
BASIC RULES FOR HAPPY PUTTING

Miss this little putt for fifteen hundred?
I should say not.

—WALTER HAGEN

**MONEY PLAYER, BEFORE SINKING
A 10-FOOTER**

Miss 'em quick!

—ALEX SMITH
**SCOTTISH-BORN PROFESSIONAL
AND WINNER OF THE 1906 AND
1910 U.S. OPENS, ON PUTTING**

Ladies and gentlemen, I three-putted
seven times this week!

—MEG MALLON

PRIOR TO TOSSING HER PUTTER
INTO THE LAKE AT WALT DISNEY
WORLD'S EAGLE PINES GOLF
COURSE, SITE OF THE 1995 LPGA
HEALTHSOUTH INAUGURAL

How do you read mud?

—TOMMY BOLT
WINNER OF THE 1958 U.S. OPEN,
COMMENTING ON POOR COURSE
CONDITIONS

But the butterflies in the stomach have hatched, and as we take our stance the line of the putt wriggles and slips around like a snake on glass. We somehow can't see it. If the putt were shorter, we would ram it in the back of the cup; longer and the break of the green would be obvious. But at this maddening in-between length, all systems break down.

—JOHN UPDIKE
WRITER AND AVID GOLFER,
ON THREE- AND FOUR-FOOTERS

Sometimes you're so into a putt that when you miss it, it's like a stab in the heart.

—TOM LEHMAN
ON MISSING A KEY EAGLE PUTT
ATTEMPT AT THE 15TH HOLE
DURING THE FINAL ROUND OF
THE 1994 MASTERS

What train?

—JOYCE WETHERED

WHEN CONGRATULATED FOR HER
IMPERTURBABILITY AFTER HOLING
A PUTT ON THE SEVENTEENTH TO
CLOSE OUT CECIL LEITCH, 2 AND 1,
IN THE 1920 ENGLISH LADIES'
CHAMPIONSHIP, WHILE A TRAIN
WAS CHUGGING BY

On the 17th and 18th greens of the regulation playoff, Els holed devilish putts on top of Roberts that could only have been made by a fearless 24-year-old or a blockhead who didn't know better.

—DAN JENKINS

GOLF WRITER, EXPLAINING HOW
ERNIE ELS' AND LOREN ROBERTS'
PUTTING KEPT THEM IN THE 1994
U.S. OPEN PLAYOFF AT OAKMONT

My putting is just ugly. I'm really down on myself.
I could have gone out there one-handed with a
wedge and done better.

> —RAYMOND FLOYD
> COMMENTING ON HIS PUTTING
> IN THE 1994 BANK OF BOSTON
> CLASSIC

A man was convicted of killing his wife of thirty years by bludgeoning her to death with a golf club. During the man's trial, prosecutors showed how the wounds on the woman's head matched the outline of the man's Ping putter.

—*GOLF DIGEST*
FEBRUARY 1995

I had 38 putts. It hurts. Deep inside it hurts. Those three putts killed me. But I still believe I'm capable of winning another Open . . . Sometimes you lose your desire through the years. Any golfer goes through that. When you play golf for a living, like anything in life, you are never going to be constant, at the top.

—TOM WATSON

WINNER OF FIVE BRITISH OPENS, AT THE 1994 OPEN AT TURNBERRY

I wasn't scared at the British. I didn't step down. I stayed strong. When I think back, there were a lot of testy putts, four or five on the front, and I holed all of them. You know, in putting, it isn't so much the break as the speed. It's who wants to win. Pure will power, I think. . . .

—JESPER PARNEVIK
RUNNERUP AT THE 1994 BRITISH OPEN, DESCRIBING THE PUTTING CONDITIONS

He was a magnificent putter, standing straight up, noticeably far from the ball, and hitting it straight in. It really looked as if the ball knew better than to disobey him.

—BERNARD DARWIN
COMMENTING ON BRITISH GOLFER
MURE FERGUSON'S PUTTING STYLE

. . . while with long strokes and short
  strokes we tend to the goal,

And with put well directed right
  into the hole

—ANONYMOUS

SONG IN PRAISE OF GOLF (1793),
THOMAS MATHISON'S 3RD EDITION
OF *THE GOFF*, THE FIRST BOOK
ON GOLF

ON
MEN'S
TOURS

The feeling toward the golf professionals in this country was such that the winner of the 1898 U.S. Open, Fred Herd, was required to put up security for the safe keeping of the trophy. It was feared he would pawn the trophy for drinking money.

—AL BARKOW
AMERICAN GOLF WRITER,
ON THE EARLY LACK OF RESPECT
FOR GOLF PROFESSIONALS

Pro golf is a parasitical business and they can do without us.

—WALTER HAGEN
**WINNER OF TWO U.S. OPENS,
FIVE PGA CHAMPIONSHIPS,
AND FOUR BRITISH OPENS**

The fastest driver was Craig Wood. He had a 12-cylinder Packard, a big, long car with two seats. He was driving fast at night in Texas with Vic Ghezzi once and drove right under a horse. He was going so fast that it pitched the horse over the car, and it didn't hurt them. It killed the horse, but only damaged the front of the car.

—PAUL RUNYAN
**DESCRIBING TRAVEL ON
THE PRO CIRCUIT IN THE 1930S**

If it were not for you Walter, this dinner would be downstairs in the pro shop and not in the ballroom.

—ARNOLD PALMER
TO WALTER HAGEN, AT A DINNER
IN HAGEN'S HONOR IN THE 1960S

In those days, the money was the main thing, the only thing I played for. Titles were something to grow old with.

—BYRON NELSON

ON PLAYING TO WIN IN
THE 1937 MASTERS

I got my golfing education from the drubbings. And very lately I have come to a sort of Presbyterian attitude toward tournament golf; I can't get away from the idea of predestination.

—BOBBY JONES
IN HIS AUTOBIOGRAPHY *DOWN THE FAIRWAY*, PUBLISHED IN 1927 WHEN HE WAS 25 YEARS OLD

Expert golf is an art, not a trade, and unionization of players doesn't work.

—BOB HARLOW
EARLY PGA TOUR DIRECTOR,
REACTING TO THE ORGANIZATION
OF PROFESSIONALS IN 1936

When a man stands alone on the tee, surrounded by galleries he knows hold him in awe because of his talent at the bewildering game of golf and also because of his willingness to risk abject failure right out in the open, he very easily, very naturally sees himself as a hero figure.

—AL BARKOW
IN HIS BOOK
GOLF'S GOLDEN GRIND

The only emotion Ben shows in defeat is surprise. You see, he expects to win.

—JIMMY DEMARET
COMMENTING ON HIS FRIEND
BEN HOGAN

If I can't play this last nine in thirty-seven strokes, I'm just a bum and don't deserve to win the Open.

—RALPH GULDAHL'S
THOUGHTS AT THE TURN BEFORE
WINNING THE 1937 U.S. OPEN

My God. I've won the Open.

—KEN VENTURI

**AFTER WINNING
THE 1964 U.S. OPEN**

Okay. But you better win this tournament . . . or else.

—LLOYD MANGRUM'S WIFE TO HER
HUBBY BEFORE THE 1946 U.S.
OPEN, AFTER CATCHING MANGRUM
IN BED WITH ANOTHER WOMAN.
LLOYD WON THE TOURNAMENT.

. . . Well, he wasn't married when he was on the Tour.

—BARBARA NICKLAUS
EXPLAINING A TOUR
PLAYER'S DEMISE

What a stupid I am.

—ROBERTO DE VICENZO
AFTER HANDING IN
AN INCORRECT SCORECARD
WHICH COST HIM
A 1968 MASTER'S WIN
BY ONE STROKE

I was tryin' to get so far ahead I could choke and still win, but I had to keep on playin'.

—LEE TREVINO
ON BEING CHASED BY
JACK NICKLAUS IN
THE 1968 U.S. OPEN.
TREVINO WON WITH
FOUR SUBPAR ROUNDS.

If you don't shut up, I'm going to tell where you swam across the border.

—DOUG SANDERS
TO A TALKATIVE LEE TREVINO
AT THE MASTERS

Do you know how many times I've had some guy on a Toro lawnmower on my butt as the sun is going down and I'm trying to make a six-footer to make the cut?

—DENNIS TRIXLER

JOURNEYMAN GOLFER

Whenever there are winners, there must be losers. In golf the winner is the man who brings in the lowest score, in stroke play, or who scores lower on more holes than his opponent, in match play. Nine times out of ten, scores are very just bases on which to judge the respective merits of golfers.

—HERBERT WARREN WIND
IN HIS BOOK *THE STORY OF AMERICAN GOLF*

You're embarrassed. You're in a fog.
You're standing in front of the
world and it's like you're playing
the hole naked.

—TOM WEISKOPF

DESCRIBING HIS THOUGHT
PROCESSES ON THE WAY TO A
13 ON THE 155-YARD PAR-5
TWELFTH AT AUGUSTA NATIONAL
IN THE 1980 MASTERS

When Christ arose God placed the Masters jacket on him.

—SIGN AT THE WOODLAWN BAPTIST CHURCH IN AUGUSTA, GEORGIA, 1972

I played 36 holes today with a kid who should have won this Open by ten shots.

—BEN HOGAN
ASSESSING JACK NICKLAUS,
A 20-YEAR-OLD AMATEUR WHO
ALMOST WON THE 1960 U.S. OPEN

I kept getting tears in my eyes. It happened to me once at Baltusrol. But here, it happened to me four or five times. I had to say to myself, Hey, you've got some golf to play.

—JACK NICKLAUS
IN THE 1986 MASTERS

I finally found that guy I used to know on the golf course. It was me.

—JACK NICKLAUS

**AFTER WINNING HIS SIXTH
MASTERS IN 1986,
AT THE AGE OF 46**

But there is a constant truth about tournament golf. Other men have to lose a championship before one man can win it.

—DAN JENKINS
GOLF WRITER

Golf pros, almost to a man are conservative. Perhaps this is forced on them by the game they play. Golf is a game of considered judgment, careful ball placement and strategy, the avoidance of hazards. Most who play are not prone to take chances.

—AL BARKOW
**GOLF WRITER,
COMMENTING ON THE
NATURE OF THE TOUR**

I'm gonna be a Spaniard
instead of a Mexkin as soon
as I get some more money.

—LEE TREVINO

JUST BEFORE WINNING HIS
FIRST U.S. OPEN IN 1968

I probably wouldn't have gone if not for the golf scholarship. Got to admit. I just walked through school as a conduit to the Tour.

—CHARLES COODY
REGARDING THE MERITS OF ATTENDING TEXAS CHRISTIAN UNIVERSITY

All you got out there is a bunch of authors and haberdashers. All you got to do to write a book is win one tournament. All of a sudden, you're telling everybody where the Vs ought to point. And them that don't win, they're haberdashers. They sell sweaters and slacks and call themselves pros.

—GEORGE LOW
OCCASIONAL GOLF PRO
AND HUSTLER

I played horrible and putted just as bad. On the back nine I had an opportunity to put everybody away, and I just didn't do it. The only consolation is that I didn't lose the tournament.

—CURTIS STRANGE

ON HIS WAY TO WINNING THE 1988
U.S. OPEN IN A PLAYOFF AGAINST
NICK FALDO

When you've got a 20-year-old daughter, you'd like to think she is going to date someone of Justin's quality. But I've been trying to get him out of my house all summer long.

—LANNY WADKINS

WINNER OF OVER $6 MILLION ON THE TOUR, COMMENTING ON FELLOW PGA COMPETITOR JUSTIN LEONARD

They must have been embarrassed
that I won, because they canceled the
tournament the next year.

> —GARY MCCORD
> **AFTER THE HOGAN TOUR
> CANCELED THE GATEWAY OPEN,
> WHICH HE WON IN 1992**

The ego is everything. And if you can't get that pumped up regularly, you can't last.

—DAVE MARR
JOURNEYMAN TOUR PLAYER

I'm not smart enough to figure out if it's good for the game or not.

—FRED COUPLES

**ON THE PROPOSED WORLD TOUR
ADVOCATED BY GREG NORMAN
AND FOX TELEVISION IN 1994**

I play golf so I can fly. At $2 a gallon for fuel, I have to support my habit somehow.

—BILL GLASSON

WHO JOINED THE TOUR IN 1984

It's great knowing how heavy
the Wanamaker Trophy is.

—PAUL AZINGER
AFTER WINNING HIS FIRST MAJOR
TOURNAMENT, THE 1993 PGA
CHAMPIONSHIP, TWO DAYS AFTER
LEARNING HE HAD CANCER

In fishing terms, this was a mackerel in the moonlight—shining one minute, smelly the next.

—GREG NORMAN

COMMENTING ON HIS "UGLY" 1-OVER-PAR WIN IN THE 1993 PGA GRAND SLAM

Those little bastards have no idea how hard we worked and how little money we made. We made the Tour what it is today and they don't even know it.

—JERRY BARBER

COMMENTING ON YOUNGER
PGA TOUR PLAYERS

Because once you sit on your ass, you die. I've got to keep active. It's what keeps me young, keeps me going to the gymnasium, setting goals for myself in business and in life. It's all part of my life—traveling, meeting people. That's the big thing. I love people. I love traveling, so I've got to keep going.

—GARY PLAYER

SENIOR TOUR PROFESSIONAL AND WINNER OF MORE THAN 125 TOURNAMENTS WORLDWIDE

If you drink, quit. If you smoke, cut down. That covers the physical end of it. Then you've got to get your brain in shape, which is even harder to do and more important. Following the same routine every week—play Wednesday through Sunday, do your laundry on Monday, travel on Tuesday—burns a lot of guys out. Forget about hitting balls, it's the lifestyle that will get you.

—LEE TREVINO
ON JOINING THE SENIOR TOUR

John Daly should crawl under the rock he came from. He doesn't realize it doesn't take much to tear down what it took Arnold Palmer and Jack Nicklaus and others 35 years to build.

—CURTIS STRANGE
IN 1994, REACTING TO JOHN DALY'S CHARGES THAT PGA TOUR PLAYERS USE DRUGS

My ultimate ambition is to be able to afford to retire from the game because it drives me berserk.

—DAVID FEHERTY
JOURNEYMAN PRO AND
GOLF COMMENTATOR

I was so far away I thought
I was in Massachusetts.

—JUSTIN LEONARD
IN HIS ROOKIE YEAR, AFTER A
PARKING LOT ATTENDANT,
REFUSING TO BELIEVE HE WAS A
COMPETITOR IN THE GREATER
HARTFORD OPEN, MADE HIM PARK
IN THE SPECTATOR'S PARKING LOT

She thinks people are crazy to complain about the Tour life. She said, "You don't have to cook, make beds, or clean houses—it's great."

—LOREN ROBERTS
EXPLAINING HIS WIFE'S ATTITUDE
TOWARD THE TOUR

It all comes back to the all-exempt Tour. It ruined the game. . . . If you miss a cut and have to qualify to play the next week, it's a whole different ball game. Half of them making more than $100,000 a year would be back home.

—BOB DRUM
GOLF WRITER, IN 1994

More camaraderie as a whole in the big group. There weren't that many players. A lot of them played tour in the winter and had a club job. It was basically a two-pro system. It wasn't as big a business as it is today.

—RAYMOND FLOYD
DISCUSSING HIS EARLY DAYS ON THE TOUR,
GOLF DIGEST **(1994)**

Arnold Palmer, I think, put his finger on why American golf has declined. The American professional tour, he says, makes it too easy for golfers to earn a living. No longer do they play to win, they play to get a good paycheck. . . . The great champions, like Palmer and Nicklaus, cared more about winning.

—MARK MCCORMACK
FOUNDER OF INTERNATIONAL
MANAGEMENT

You made all this possible,
Arnold. We're all here because
of you.

—ROCCO MEDIATE
TO FELLOW PROFESSIONAL
ARNOLD PALMER AFTER ARNIE
FINISHED HIS LAST U.S. OPEN
AT OAKMONT IN 1994

He's going to win more of these [Master's titles] than Arnold [Palmer] and I combined.

—JACK NICKLAUS

AFTER PLAYING A PRACTICE ROUND WITH TIGER WOODS AT THE MASTERS IN 1996

In the case of all game players, year-books and books of scores are the only things to count in the long run, when the time of living memory is past: the names of "uncrowned kings" are apt to fade and be forgotten.

—BERNARD DARWIN

ON GOLFERS WHO FAIL TO WIN CHAMPIONSHIPS

ON
WOMEN'S
TOURS

Indoor golf is to be one of the features of the athletic work of many young society girls this winter. They are the younger girls, hardly risen to the dignity of society "buds," but they have already been exposed to the contagion of golf, and they will prepare this winter to be genuine fanatics by the time their school duties are over.

—THE *NEW YORK TIMES*
NOVEMBER 14, 1897

Nancy, I don't want the money if I have to make it this way. I want to live my life outdoors. I want to play golf.

—BABE ZAHARIAS
TO HER SISTER ESTHER NANCY,
ON DECIDING TO GIVE UP A
$2,500-PER-WEEK DEPRESSION-
ERA VAUDEVILLE CONTRACT
TO PLAY COMPETITIVE GOLF

Babe Zaharias was a remarkable person. She was no pantywaist, I'll tell you. She definitely was stronger than most men. When she walked, her muscles just rippled under her skin. She could hit it longer than I could; so could Mickey Wright.

—PAUL RUNYON
WINNER OF 28 PGA TOURNAMENTS

I worked for my money, why shouldn't they? Why should I support them now—if I get sick, are they going to feel an obligation to support me?

—LOUISE SUGGS

LPGA PROFESSIONAL, IN 1961,
EXPRESSING HER OPPOSITION
TO SHARING PURSES (5 PERCENT)
WITH GOLFERS OUT OF THE
MONEY IN A TOURNAMENT

I found two sharks. They were washed up on the beach, and I tried to cut them open with my pocket knife, but they were too tough, so I took the car and ran over them, but that didn't work either. I mean I never saw the inside of a shark.

—CAROL MANN
LPGA GOLFER, RECALLING
TOUR ADVENTURES ALONG THE
GULF OF MEXICO IN THE 1960S

I wonder what they think about women and children. They seem so lonely. Nothing to look forward to, to come home to.

—MURLE MACKENZIE
LPGA PROFESSIONAL,
COMMENTING ON
THE EARLY LPGA TOUR

It is my belief that this attitude of aggressiveness is far more prevalent in competitive golf today than it used to be. It creates poor sportsmanship and spoils the joy of the game for the players and the pleasures of watching a shot-making game for the gallery.

—VIRGINIA VAN WIE
THREE-TIME U.S. AMATEUR
CHAMPION (1932–34),
COMMENTING ON WOMEN'S
COMPETITIVE GOLF IN THE
AMERICAN GOLFER MAGAZINE
(1934)

I remember making rulings on other players in a tournament I was competing in. In this day and age, you'd probably get sued for something like that.

—BETSY RAWLS

WINNER OF 55 LPGA EVENTS AND A MEMBER OF THE LPGA HALL OF FAME, RECALLING THE FORMATIVE YEARS OF THE TOUR WHEN SHE WAS AN LPGA EXECUTIVE

Winning the Open is the greatest thing in golf. I have come close before. This time I'd thought I'd won. But I didn't. Golf is played by the rules, and I broke a rule. I've learned a lesson. And I have two broad shoulders.

—JACKIE PUNG

AFTER BEING DISQUALIFIED
IN THE 1957 U.S. WOMEN'S OPEN
AT WINGED FOOT WHERE SHE
REPORTED A CORRECT TOTAL
SCORE BUT RECORDED AN
INCORRECT SCORE ON ONE HOLE

I thought you had to be
dead to win that.

—JOANNE CARNER
LPGA HALL OF FAMER, IN 1982,
ON WINNING THE BOB JONES
AWARD FOR SPORTSMANSHIP

Golf is my job and that motivates me. I have a talent. I want to develop it. Every year I learn a different shot. That's what great about golf. It's a very complex game, very challenging. You never stop learning.

—BETSY KING
WINNER OF OVER $5 MILLION ON THE LPGA TOUR

Well it just goes to show what we've been saying all along. That all the good-looking golfers are on the ladies' tour.

—JAN STEPHENSON
RESPONDING TO A GOLF
MAGAZINE CENTERFOLD
ON MALE PGA TOUR GOLFERS

I felt something heavy. It was not that I was not feeling well. Maybe you could call it pressure.

—AYAKO OKOMOTO

IN 1988, AFTER FAILING TO WIN THE MAZDA-PGA CHAMPIONSHIP

She's like a shark. I would love to be in her body, just one time, to feel exactly what she feels. Just when she gets to a point you think nerves could bother her, she gets right past it.

—HENRI REIS

LONGTIME COACH OF ANNIKA SORENSTAM, WHO HAS WON THREE U.S. OPENS, THREE KRAFT NABISCOS, THREE LPGA CHAMPIONSHIPS, AND ONE BRITISH OPEN, ALL MODERN WOMEN'S MAJOR TOURNAMENTS

I started in engineering and switched to business for my major. If I had stayed for my junior year, I'd have had to switch to basket weaving. It was getting tough.

—NANCY LOPEZ
RECALLING HOW SHE LEFT
TULSA UNIVERSITY TO JOIN
THE LPGA TOUR

Having a good time is winning the tournament.

—JAN STEPHENSON
WINNER OF 16 LPGA EVENTS

I didn't have to deal with that kind of subjectivity (e.g., Baseball Hall of Fame balloting). I was Pat Bradley, Hall-of-Famer, the moment I won my thirtieth.

—PAT BRADLEY
WHO PLAYED HER WAY INTO THE
LPGA HALL OF FAME WITH THIRTY
WINS, INCLUDING TWO MAJORS

I used to sling the old golf club quite a distance. Tony (my brother) and I used to be dreadful. We would spend twenty minutes or longer trying to retrieve a club one of us had thrown into a tree.

—LAURA DAVIES
NATIVE OF COVENTRY, ENGLAND, AND LPGA TOUR PLAYER

Dad, I won. I really
played well today.
Happy father's day!

—NANCY LOPEZ

**CALLING HOME AFTER WINNING A
RECORD FIFTH STRAIGHT LPGA
EVENT IN 1978, HER ROOKIE YEAR**

One player asked me,
"Who's Mickey Wright?"
I felt like slapping her.

—KATHY POSTELWAIT

IN 1993, AT MICKEY WRIGHT'S FIRST
TOURNAMENT IN EIGHT YEARS,
THE SPRING SENIOR CHALLENGE

Everyone has a dream. Mine was America, where everything seems to be number one. In Japan, I started to be a superstar, but I didn't want to be famous. Back home no star has privacy. If you have a hole in your jeans, everyone wants to know why. Here in America, nobody cares.

—AYAKO OKOMOTO
ON WHY SHE JOINED
THE LPGA TOUR

All I was thinking was that I didn't have anything to wear the next day. I thought I was going to have to do laundry that night, especially after Helen [Alfredsson] hit her shot at 18. She nearly flew it into the hole.

—LAURIE MERTEN

1993 U.S. WOMEN'S OPEN CHAMPION, RECALLING HER THOUGHTS IN THE FINAL ROUND, ANTICIPATING A PLAYOFF

They thought I was somebody just walking, hanging out in the rough.

—HELEN ALFREDSSON
CONTENDER IN THE 1994 U.S. WOMEN'S OPEN, COMMENTING ON HOW A MARSHAL MISTOOK HER FOR A SPECTATOR

I had a strange feeling. I do remember walking down the 15th fairway, which has always been something of a turning point in the event [the Nabisco Dinah Shore]. I had a weird sensation that it was my tournament to win. It was strange, because under normal circumstances you feel like throwing up.

—DOTTIE MOCHRIE

ON WINNING THE 1992 NABISCO DINAH SHORE, AND LPGA MAJOR

It's nice to be well liked, but it's even better to be well liked and respected.

—MEG MALLON

**WINNER OF THE 1991
U.S. WOMEN'S OPEN,
AFTER BEING NAMED THE LPGA'S
"MOST POPULAR PLAYER" IN 1990**

When I finally quit, for the first time in my life I am going to unpack everything, get all of my clothes pressed, and put them on hangers. I used to love the Tour when I first started because I didn't have to make my own bed. Now I hate living in motels. I want to come home.

—NANCY LOPEZ
IN 1984, AFTER HAVING HER FIRST CHILD

We'll either hire someone to travel with me or my mom will do it. Just because you've had a baby doesn't mean you can't win tournaments. Nancy Lopez proved that.

—JULIE INKSTER
IN 1989, EXPLAINING HOW
SHE WILL HANDLE COMPETITIVE
GOLF AND MOTHERHOOD

Adeline was looking up at him tenderly. "May I come, too, and walk round with you?" Cuthbert's bosom heaved, "Oh," he said, with a tremor in his voice, "that you would walk round with me for life!"

—P. G. WODEHOUSE
THE CLICKING OF CUTHBERT **(1922)**

All you had to do was look at her. She has all the ability in the world. She can drive, chip, putt. All her shots are top class. And her temperament. She's an ice-cool Swede, one of the best talents in the world.

—LAURA DAVIES
ASSESSING ANIKA SORENSTAM'S TALENT

It's definitely been a learning experience, not just in golf but in general. The biggest adjustment has been not knowing where I'm going, how I'm going to get there . . . and when I get to a new town it seems as though I get lost every time.

—VICKI GOETZE

WINNER OF THE 1989 AND 1992 U.S. WOMEN'S AMATEUR AND THE 1992 NCAA CHAMPIONSHIP, ADJUSTING TO THE TOUR

I'm coming home and I'm bringing home the trophy and it's a big one.

—JULIE INKSTER
TO HER DAUGHTERS,
AFTER WINNING THE 1999
U.S. WOMEN'S OPEN

ON
CADDIES

A day of clubs, a silver town or two,

A flask of scotch, a pipe of shag—
and thou

Beside me caddying in the wilderness—

Ah, wilderness were paradise enow

—H. W. BOYNTON
IN THE *GOLFER'S RUBAIYAT*

The player may experiment about with his swing, his grip, his stance. It is only when he begins asking his caddies' advice that he is getting on dangerous ground.

—SIR WALTER SIMPSON
IN HIS BOOK *THE ART OF GOLF*
(1887)

The professional [caddie] is a reckless, feckless creature. In the golfing season in Scotland he makes money all the day and spends it all the night. His sole loves are golf and whiskey.

—HORACE HUTCHINSON
GOLF WRITER AND GOLFER,
IN 1900

. . . It is not impossible that the caddie knows less about the game than yourself, and, on the other hand, his views as to the best thing to do in a particular situation are often regulated by what he has seen the scratch men do at such times. You may not be a scratch man.

—HARRY VARDON
IN HIS BOOK *SOME GENERAL HINTS*

One time the caddies talked of a strike unless wages were raised. Ross heard of this, walked to the caddie pen, and asked the leader what was going on. Hearing the grievance, he whacked the caddie on the head with his everpresent five-iron and informed him the strike was over.

—ROD INNES

REMEMBERING NOTED GOLF ARCHITECT DONALD ROSS AT EARLY 20TH-CENTURY PINEHURST, IN THE BOOK *PINEHURST STORIES* (1991) BY LEE PACE

There are three things in the world that he held in the smallest esteem—slugs, poets and caddies with hiccups.

—P. G. WODEHOUSE
IN "RODNEY FAILS TO QUALIFY"
(1924)

Look here, sir. I'll give
you the club, you play
the bloody shot.

—WILLIE BLACK

**MUIRFIELD CADDIE,
TO BOBBY CRUICKSHANK
IN 1925**

It'll take three good ones to be on in two t'day sir.

—A CADDIE TO HENRY LONGHURST,
PLAYING INTO A STIFF WIND

You know Deane Beman? When he han'
the money out, he look at you like you
done stab him in the knee.

—A CADDIE'S REMARKS
 IN GEORGE PLIMPTON'S ESSAY
 "THEY ALSO SERVE"

Why ask me? You've asked me two times already and paid no attention to what I said. Pick your own club.

—DOW FINSTERWALD'S CADDIE,
IN THE 1960 U.S. OPEN

Very few caddies make good tees. The ball should be just perched on the sand so that none of the latter can be seen. . . .

—HARRY VARDON
IN *HOW TO PLAY GOLF*
(CA. 1912, IN THE DAYS BEFORE
MANUFACTURED TEES)

It was one of the greatest thrills of my life. I remember she was wearing tennis shoes and outdistancing the other ladies by twenty yards.

—PAUL AZINGER
RECALLING THE TIME HE CADDIED FOR MICKEY WRIGHT

I know you can be fined for throwing a club, but I want to know if you can get fined for throwing a caddie?

—**TOMMY BOLT**
WINNER OF 11 PGA TOUR EVENTS

If a permanent caddie is heroin, if you're going to break out in a cold sweat because you don't have him, then you'd better get one.

—FRANK BEARD
U.S. SENIOR TOUR PLAYER

. . . Better tournament golf scoring
was particularly due to the Depression
because it induced thousands of urchins
who might otherwise have been playing
baseball or annoying their parents to
earn an honest dollar by caddying.

—NOEL F. BUSH
IN *THE NEW YORKER* IN 1937

How much money do I have?
If I knew I wouldn't have very
much, would I?

—JOE JEMSEK
FORMER DEPRESSION-ERA CADDIE
WHO BECAME OWNER OF COG HILL
AND OTHER FINE GOLF COURSES
IN THE CHICAGO AREA

It is a game of tradition, one we'd like to maintain. Plus, I don't think their long legs look very good.

—REG MURPHY

USGA PRESIDENT, EXPLAINING WHY HE DECLINED TO ALLOW CADDIES TO WEAR SHORTS DURING THE SEARING HEAT OF THE 1994 U.S. OPEN AT OAKMONT

All you've got is your bag carriers now. All they can do is give the golfer a weather report— not the right club.

—ALFIE

TOM WATSON'S CADDIE, AT THE 1977 BRITISH OPEN AT TURNBERRY

Shots like that are a little too much for a 24-year-old heart, Dad.

—CADDIE JACKIE NICKLAUS
TO HIS FATHER JACK, AFTER HE
ALMOST PUT HIS TEE SHOT INTO
RAE'S CREEK ON THE PAR-3
THIRTEENTH DURING THE FINAL
ROUND OF THE 1986 MASTERS

Here boy, give me the bag.
I'll go down the fairway and
you stay here and find the
ball. You'd better find it, too,
or don't come back.

—MR. ERICKSON PERKINS
A PROMINENT ROCHESTER
BANKER, TO WALTER HAGEN
DURING HIS CADDIE DAYS

If a caddie can help you, then you don't know how to play golf.

—DAN JENKINS
IN HIS BOOK *DEAD SOLID PERFECT*

ON
MATCHES

I play golf with friends but we don't play friendly golf.

—BEN HOGAN

When making a match, do not try to get a greater allowance of strokes than that to which you are entitled on your handicap, alleging to your opponent that the said handicap is an unfair one. Your opponent may think you are a little too "keen"; and if he grants your improper request, and you should win the match, he may think some other things besides.

—HARRY VARDON
FROM *SOME GENERAL HINTS*

What is love compared with holing out before your opponent?

—P. G. WODEHOUSE

He smiles as he plays, but it is not a broad smile, just a faint flicker over his features. It is what you might call the Vardonic Smile. He was never a worrier, or recounter of lost strokes. Nothing ruffled him. He sank into the game but there was nothing grim about him. No teeth grinding or setting of jaw.

—ANDREW KIRKALDY
BRITISH GOLF PROFESSIONAL,
RECALLING HARRY VARDON

My dad always told me, "Don't lift weights, you will lose your feel and your touch." David and Tiger have proven that you can keep your swing and keep your touch, and they are better, stronger golfers for it.

—DAVIS LOVE III

COMMENTING ON THE CONDITIONING PROGRAMS OF PGA TOUR RIVALS TIGER WOODS AND DAVID DUVAL IN 2000

I've heard players speak proudly of fifth-place finishes. If you can be happy with fifth, it could be that you don't have what it takes to win.

—MICKEY WRIGHT
WINNER OF 82 LPGA EVENTS,
COMMENTING ON
THE LPGA TOUR IN 1976

I know how to choke. Given even a splinter-thin opportunity to let my side down and destroy my own score, I will seize it. Not only does ice water not run through my veins, but what runs there has a boiling point lower than body temperature.

—JOHN UPDIKE
IN *GOLF DIGEST* **IN 1995**

I'm a guy who'll play with amateurs. A $50 Nassau, $500, $5,000 or nothing. It doesn't matter. I just like to play.

—LEE TREVINO
IN *GOLF DIGEST* IN 1994

My girls were getting close to college age. And that was the main reason I did it. They needed some more money for school.

—ALLEN DOYLE

IN 1999, ON WHY HE JOINED THE SENIOR TOUR

I think professional golfers are the most competitive athletes of all. Every time out, we play against the whole league. The league never has a bad day either.

—JIM COLBERT
WINNER OF 8 PGA TOUR EVENTS
AND OVER $3 MILLION ON
THE SENIOR TOUR

I have not played golf with anyone, man or woman, amateur or professional, who made me feel so utterly outclassed.

—BOBBY JONES
COMMENTING ON
JOYCE WETHERED

He didn't beat me,
sir. I beat myself,
I beat myself.

—J. H. TAYLOR
**WINNER OF FIVE BRITISH OPENS
(1894–95, 1900, 1909, 1913),
AFTER LOSING A MATCH**

Never bet with anyone you meet on
the first tee who has a deep suntan, a
one-iron in his bag, and squinty eyes.

—DAVE MARR
**WINNER OF THE 1965
PGA CHAMPIONSHIP**

The lord hates a coward.

—BYRON NELSON
TO HIMSELF DURING HIS
1937 MASTERS WIN

Who the hell was that?

—BEN HOGAN

**REACTING TO A SKIED 100-YARD
DRIVE BY BOB TOSKI**

When things headed south, he wasn't the Mickelson we had often seen in the past, who could vanish from a leader board in an instant. He fought back righting the ship. Asked the best part of Mickelson's game over the entire week, his longtime caddie and close friend, Jim "Bones" McKay, answered instantly.

"Guts," he said. "He showed a lot of heart."

—JEFF BABINEAU
WRITING IN *GOLFWEEK* IN HIS PIECE,
"DIAMOND IN THE ROUGH," ABOUT
PHIL MICKELSON'S SECOND MAJOR
TOURNAMENT WIN, THE U.S. OPEN AT
BALTUSROL IN 2006

Why don't you come down here and play me! Come on, come on. You and your kid too. I'll give you two a side and play your low ball.

—TOMMY BOLT
**CONVERSING WITH GOD,
AFTER MISSING A SHORT PUTT**

To anyone else, perhaps the fact that I had beaten Cecil Leitch was unimportant—an off-day for the champion. To me it was the beginning of a successful career. I had gained confidence I needed so badly. My nerves became steadier, my shot bolder. No opponent held any terror for me.

—GLENNA COLLETT
AFTER DEFEATING CECIL LEITCH
1-UP IN THE BERTHELLY CUP
MATCHES AT THE HUNTINGTON
VALLEY COUNTRY CLUB NEAR
PHILADELPHIA IN 1921

The one thing that Hogan and Snead and I had in common was that we wanted to beat somebody.

—BYRON NELSON

Hey, I won three times and I never even got an outhouse.

—JIMMY DEMARET
THE FIRST THREE-TIME MASTERS
WINNER, COMMENTING ON
BRIDGES BUILT TO HONOR
GENE SARAZEN AND BYRON
NELSON AT AUGUSTA NATIONAL

Give me a man with a fast backswing and a fat wallet.

—GOLF HUSTLER'S ANCIENT SLOGAN

Then came the playoff. This was one of the rare occasions when I was so keyed up my stomach was upset, even during the night. I lost my breakfast the next morning, which I thought might be a good sign because I had always played well when I became that sick beforehand.

—BYRON NELSON

BEFORE HIS 18-HOLE PLAYOFF WIN, 69–70, AGAINST BEN HOGAN IN THE 1942 MASTERS

I guess I must have choked.

—BERT YANCEY

**AFTER A FINAL ROUND SCORE
OF 76 COST HIM THE 1968
U.S. OPEN CHAMPIONSHIP**

. . . [Great players] learn that they don't need to play their best golf to win. They only need to shoot the lowest score.

—RICK REILLY
SPORTS WRITER,
IN HIS ESSAY "BANK SHOT"

I key myself to when I'm in contention coming down to those last few holes. It is a miserable, sick, lonely feeling. You're so scared, sometimes you can't see. But when I can pull off a good shot on those holes, that's what I look forward to. And I figure I haven't won nearly enough.

—SANDRA PALMER
WINNER OF 21 LPGA EVENTS

When their names are mentioned, which is all too infrequently, there is almost invariably a shade of sadness that accompanies names of men who are remembered not as winners but as losers.

—HERBERT WARREN WIND

COMMENTING ON MACDONALD SMITH, LEO DIEGEL AND HARRY COPPER, EXCELLENT SHOTMAKERS, GOLFER'S GOLFERS, WHO NEVER WON A NATIONAL CHAMPIONSHIP

Forget it. I can beat any two players in this tournament by myself. If I need any help, I'll let you know.

—BABE ZAHARIAS
REASSURING HER PARTNER PEGGY KIRK BELL, WHO WAS NERVOUS AT THE START OF A FOUR-BALL EVENT

Qualifying competitions are dull
things unless they are cruel.

—BERNARD DARWIN

BRITISH GOLF JOURNALIST AND
MEMBER OF BRITAIN'S FIRST
WALKER CUP TEAM IN 1922

Clues of his greatness came early and often. Certainly no golf toddler had appeared before on the Mike Douglas Show or had won three U.S. Juniors in a row. And never had a young man completed a U.S. Amateur Trifecta.

—GENE YASUDA

IN HIS PIECE "TIGER'S IMPACT" IN A GOLFWEEK REGARDING THE EARLY TIGER WOODS

I'm terrible! No one could be two up on the 16th and lose.

—LAURA BAUGH

TO HER FATHER, AFTER LOSING OUT TO HOLLIS STACEY IN THE 1971 U.S. GIRLS' JUNIOR

Because that's how goddamn good
Bobby Jones was.

It may not be out of place here to say that I never won a major championship until I learned to play golf against something, not somebody. And that something was par.

—BOBBY JONES
WINNER OF THE U.S. OPEN,
THE U.S. AMATEUR, THE BRITISH
OPEN, AND THE BRITISH AMATEUR
IN 1930, MAKING HIM THE ONLY
PLAYER TO WIN THE "GRAND
SLAM" IN A SINGLE YEAR

Q: Are you a golfer?

A: I don't think so but I believe that they will want me inside to receive the championship cup.

—DOROTHY HURD'S
REPLY TO AN OFFICIAL BLOCKING
HER WAY TO THE AWARDS
CEREMONY AFTER SHE WON
THE 1909 BRITISH LADIES'
CHAMPIONSHIP AT BIRKDALE

When I grew up there was always a wager. It was just part of the fabric of the game. We'd play for nickels, dimes, and quarters on the putting green. I realized, even at a young age, that if you got better, you could win more nickels, dimes, and quarters. It made me work that much harder.

—RAYMOND FLOYD
IN *GOLF DIGEST* **IN 1994**

If a guy says it's against his religion,
tell him to get another religion.

—LANNY WADKINS

WINNER OF THE 1977 PGA
CHAMPIONSHIP, ON GAMBLING
IN PRACTICE ROUNDS PRIOR
TO TOURNAMENTS

I just feel that the Ryder Cup, if it were left to the players, would be a wonderful event. The players would compete and have fun. It would be what it was meant to be, which is good will between two golfing organizations. The Ryder Cup has become a war . . . largely because of the press.

—JACK NICKLAUS
IN *GOLF DIGEST* IN 1991

In stroke play I don't particularly care what the guys I am playing with shoot or do, because you're just trying to play the course. In match play I think you find yourself rooting against your opponent a lot more, because the difference between winning a hole could be the difference between winning or losing the match.

—MARCH CALCAVECCHIA
IN *GOLF DIGEST* **IN 1991**

I've seen lifelong friends drift apart over golf simply because one could play better but the other counted better.

—STEPHEN LEACOCK

I've been down 6 before, but I've never been 6 down and won. You've got to stay positive, and that's all I wanted to do.

—TIGER WOODS
AFTER COMING FROM BEHIND
TO WIN THE 1994 U.S. AMATEUR

ON
COURSE
DESIGN

Gorse, a low brambly shrub of the genus ulex, is common to Scottish wastelands and golfing links. It is said by some to grow as well in the fields of hell.

—MICHAEL MURPHY
IN HIS BOOK *GOLF IN THE KINGDOM*
(1972)

The example of public-spirited park commissioners of New York . . . in providing public links in Van Cortlandt Park, is bearing good fruit.

—C. TURNER

FROM AN ARTICLE IN *THE OUTING* IN 1896 PRAISING THE OPENING OF THE FIRST MUNICIPAL PUBLIC GOLF COURSE IN THE UNITED STATES

Broadly speaking, the penal school follows more or less the methods of Tom Morris and the brothers Dunn, in scattering plenty of bunkers in places most likely to catch inaccurate shots.

—TOM SIMPSON
GOLF COURSE ARCHITECT, IN HIS
BOOK *THE GAME OF GOLF* (1931)

This is the essence of strategic architecture: to encourage initiative, reward a well-played stroke, and yet to insist that there must be planning and honest self-appraisal behind the daring.

—ROBERT TRENT JONES, SR.
**DESIGNER OF OVER
400 GOLF COURSES,
ON STRATEGIC DESIGN IN 1954**

The object of inventors is to reduce the skill required for golf. If it were not for the counterskill of architects, the game would be emasculated.

—JOHN L. LOW
A FOUNDER OF THE OXFORD
AND CAMBRIDGE GOLFING
SOCIETY IN 1897

Gentlemen, the defense rests. I think the hole is eminently fair.

—ROBERT TRENT JONES, SR.
IN 1954, RESPONDING TO CRITICISM
OF A PAR-3 HOLE AT BALTUSROL
THAT HE REDESIGNED FOR
THE U.S. OPEN, AFTER SCORING
AN ACE ON THE HOLE TO
ILLUSTRATE HIS POINT

Saw a course you'd really like, Trent. On the first tee you drop the ball over your left shoulder.

—JIMMY DEMARET
TO ROBERT TRENT JONES, SR.,
DESIGNER OF SPYGLASS HILL,
MAUNA KEA, FIRESTONE. AND
MANY OTHER COURSES

Wind and rain are great challenges. They separate the real golfers. Let the seas pound against the shore, let the rain pour.

—TOM WATSON
**WINNER OF 8 MAJORS AND
32 PGA TOUR EVENTS**

Before I got out of the rough in one tournament it had turned into a shopping center.

—BOB HOPE

**ON HIS POOR PLAY IN
A PRO-AM TOURNAMENT**

I fell violently in love with Cypress Point. But I was so furious because I was so besotted with the beauty of it that I just couldn't hit a golf ball.

—ENID WILSON
MEMBER OF THE FIRST BRITISH
CURTIS CUP TEAM (1932), ON
VISITING CYPRESS POINT IN 1931

Reporter: What does it (Hazeltine) lack?

Hill: Eighty acres of corn and a few cows. They ruined a good farm when they built this course.

> —DAVE HILL'S CRITIQUE OF
> HAZELTINE AFTER THE SECOND
> ROUND OF THE 1970 U.S. OPEN

Ninety-seven percent of the field, myself included, are not equipped to play this course. We just don't have the shots. I heard Byron Nelson say on television that 272 would win here. I couldn't shoot 272 if I got a mulligan on every hole.

—GEORGE ARCHER

COMMENTING ON MERION BEFORE THE 1971 U.S. OPEN. NICKLAUS AND TREVINO TIED IN REGULATION AT 280 AND TREVINO SHOT A 68 TO WIN THE PLAYOFF BY THREE SHOTS. ARCHER SHOT 283.

I vowed that I would bring this monster to its knees.

—BEN HOGAN

**COMMENTING ON OAKLAND HILLS
AFTER HE SUCCESSFULLY
DEFENDED HIS U.S. OPEN TITLE
THERE IN 1951**

Hell, man, Ray Charles could play here . . .
and it still wouldn't make no difference.

—LEE TREVINO
DISCUSSING THE SUBTLETIES
OF MUIRFIELD DURING
THE 1972 BRITISH OPEN

Pine Valley is an examination in golf.

—BERNARD DARWIN'S APPRAISAL OF
ONE OF THE WORLD'S BEST AND
MOST DIFFICULT TESTS OF GOLF

Foursomes have left the first tee there and have never been seen again. They just find their shoelaces and bags.

—BOB HOPE
EVALUATING PINE VALLEY

I've never seen Augusta so beautiful.
If heaven is this pretty, I'd go there
tomorrow.

—GENE SARAZEN
**WINNER OF THE 1935 MASTERS,
IN 1981**

Most of the courses today, the guys shoot twenty under par and think they've accomplished something. They can't do it at PGA West because you can't hit it crooked and score. Golf was meant to be a great game of skill, not just strength. You get around here you have to have some skills.

—CHI-CHI RODRIGUEZ
ASSESSING PGA WEST

I've got no business going to the U.S. Open this week and playing a hard course like Medinah.

> —LOU GRAHAM
> **BEFORE WINNING THE 1975
> U.S. OPEN IN A PLAYOFF AGAINST
> JOHN MAHAFFEY AT MEDINAH**

. . . this is the first time in the history of golf that a course has been designed specifically to test the best female players in the game.

—GOLF ARCHITECT REES JONES
COMMENTING ON HIS RECENTLY
OPENED LPGA INTERNATIONAL
GOLF COURSE IN 1995

My God, you can get starting times in six different languages.

—THOMAS P. "TIP" O'NEILL, JR.
FORMER SPEAKER OF THE U.S.
HOUSE OF REPRESENTATIVES,
COMMENTING ON THE CAMBRIDGE,
MASSACHUSETTS, COURSE
RENAMED IN HIS HONOR AFTER
HE RETIRED FROM POLITICS

But here, the 100-player, the 80-player, the 75-player, has only one shot to play from the sand; and neither boldness nor skill will help him correct a position which may not have been his fault in the first place. He has one shot—the blast. That is all.

—TED RAY

NOTING THE UNFAIRNESS OF
OAKMONT'S FURROWED BUNKERS
DURING THE 1927 U.S. OPEN

You gotta sneak up on these holes.
Iffen you clamber and clank up on 'em,
they're liable to turn round and bite you.

—SAM SNEAD
COMMENTING ON OAKMONT,
ONE OF GOLF'S
MOST PENAL COURSES,
DURING THE 1953 U.S. OPEN

While I have never met Pete Dye, I know him well. He is 500 years old and has absorbed the wisdom of the ages. He has a pointed hat and a flowing robe embroidered with occult symbols. When he speaks, he becomes extremely animated, and gesticulates a lot with flashes of blue static crackling from his long fingernails.

—PETER DOBEREINER
ON GOLF COURSE BUILDER
PETE DYE, WHOSE COURSES
ARE SOMETIMES
CONSIDERED DIABOLICAL

Where are the windmills and animals?

—FUZZY ZOELLER

**COMMENTING ON PETE DYE'S TPC
STADIUM COURSE AT SAWGRASS**

Don't give me the excuse that you weren't standing there, and you approved it. I don't want to listen to your alibis, let's just fix the hole.

—ALICE DYE
AMATEUR GOLF CHAMPION AND THE FIRST WOMAN TO BECOME A MEMBER OF THE AMERICAN SOCIETY OF GOLF COURSE ARCHITECTS, TO HER HUSBAND PETE. ON A GOLF COURSE CONSTRUCTION SITE

I'm not going back to a place where they never rake the goddamn bunkers.

—BEN HOGAN
AFTER WINNING THE 1953
BRITISH OPEN AT CARNOUSTIE

After my first qualifying round in the 1963 British Amateur Championship, I brashly told the astonished Scottish reporter that the Old Course at St. Andrews was a goat ranch, and if I played it a thousand times it would still be a goat ranch! Three days and seven rounds later, I realized it was one of the greatest golf courses in the world.

—PETE DYE

WHO HAS INCORPORATED "OLD STYLE" ARCHITECTURAL FEATURES INTO HIS GOLF COURSE DESIGNS

I know a one-shot finishing hole is not usually well-regarded. But when a player stands on that tee at East Lake, with the match square or dormie—that drive calls for all there is in the delicatessen department.

—BOBBY JONES'S FATHER
REGARDING THE EIGHTEENTH
HOLE ON EAST LAKE NO. 1,
A 200-YARD PAR 3 ACROSS WATER

In discussing the need for simplicity of design, the chief object of every golf course architect worth his salt is to imitate the beauties of nature so closely as to make his work indistinguishable from nature itself.

—ALISTER MACKENZIE
IN HIS BOOK *GOLF ARCHITECTURE* **(1920)**

Laddie, a blind hole is blind only once to a man with a memory.

—TOMMY ARMOUR

WINNER OF 24 PGA EVENTS

Walk the course and annotate your scorecard with distances before an important match. It will save you the element of doubt as you prepare to hit your shots.

—DR. BOB ROTELLA
GOLF PSYCHOLOGIST

The average golfer is inclined to
become emotional when talking
about golf course architecture.

—RICHARD S. TUFTS
IN *GOLF DIGEST* **IN 1968**

In my experience, the decision to increase green speeds has definitely hurt the game of golf. This development has not only caused many of the greens on the great golf courses to be nearly unplayable, but has really hampered the ability of a number of players to negotiate the new speed levels.

—PETE DYE
GOLF COURSE ARCHITECT

ON
THE GAME
ABROAD

Gentlemen, this beats rifle shooting. It is a game I think might go in our country.

—AMERICAN WILLIAM K. VANDERBILT
IN BIARRITZ AT THE END
OF THE NINETEENTH CENTURY,
WHEN HE SAW WILLIE DUNN,
THE FAMOUS GOLF ARCHITECT
AND PROFESSIONAL HIT
A FEW PRACTICE SHOTS

Think of teeing off in the land where bairns cut their teeth on niblicks and brassies, and the nineteenth hole still thrives—bonny Scotland, the gowfer's paradise.

—AN AD IN *GOLF ILLUSTRATED* FOR THE WHITE STAR LINE IN 1929

Sorry, I don't play golf while on vacation.

—BEN HOGAN

**WHEN ASKED IF HE WAS
AVAILABLE TO PLAY
A ROUND OF GOLF WITH
THE KING OF BELGIUM**

What else is there to do over there? Wear a skirt?

A reasonable number of fleas is good for a dog. It keeps the dog forgetting that he is a dog.

—WALTER TRAVIS
TO FRIENDS IN REACTION
TO REAL AND IMAGINED SLIGHTS
FROM THE BRITISH, PRIOR TO
THE 1904 BRITISH AMATEUR
THAT TRAVIS WON AT SANDWICH

I'm tired of giving it
my best and not having
it be good enough.

—JACK NICKLAUS

**AFTER LOSING THE BRITISH OPEN
BY ONE SHOT AT TURNBERRY
IN 1977**

One of the prerequisites to win a major championship is to enter the damn thing. You are not going to win the British Open by correspondence.

—TOM KITE

CRITICIZING EXEMPT U.S. PLAYERS
WHO FAIL TO PLAY IN
THE BRITISH OPEN

You stop this nonsense or I'll take the Royal out of St. George's.

—THE PRINCE OF WALES
ADMONISHING A STEWARD IN THE ST. GEORGE'S CLUBHOUSE WHO CLAIMED HE COULD NOT SERVE WALTER HAGEN AND GENE SARAZEN, THE PRINCE'S GUESTS

Wee wheels in ya head sir. You've got to forget those bloody wee wheels sir.

—SANDY MATHESON
A CADDIE AT DORNOCH,
TO WRITER RICK REILLY

I hope they regret it the rest of their lives.

—INTERNATIONAL TEAM CAPTAIN
DAVID GRAHAM

**ON THE PLAYERS WHO
ELECTED NOT TO COMPETE
IN THE INAUGURAL PRESIDENT'S
CUP IN 1994**

They interested us immensely by bringing with them huge quantities of clubs and balls—the latter for practice purposes—which were carted about the countryside in the most awe-inspiring voluminous leather caddie bags. ·

—ENID WILSON
DESCRIBING THE AMERICAN
TEAM'S PREPARATION FOR
AN INFORMAL MATCH AGAINST
THE BRITISH IN 1930. THIS EVENT
FORESHADOWED THE CURTIS CUP
MATCHES, WHICH BEGAN IN 1932.

While PGA touring professionals have been brought up on manicured courses since junior golf, the foreign contingent have been raised on bad lies and rough weather requiring mental toughness.

—PETE DYE

NOTING WHY INTERNATIONAL GOLFERS HAVE REACHED PARITY WITH OR HAVE SURPASSED THE AMERICANS

We learned to play foursomes from the Americans. For years, every time we had a shot to play, we would always confer with our partner. It was sort of a cop-out, really, sharing the responsibility. The Americans never did that. Each played her own game and took responsibility for the shot.

—JOHN BAILEY
HUSBAND OF DIANE BAILEY,
CAPTAIN OF
THE 1986 CURTIS CUP TEAM

The Americans respect you more as a player. Australians don't appreciate their own players. They feel like you are a traitor to leave the country and do well. I think they are jealous. Maybe it stems from the war. Maybe people think the Americans came over, met the prettiest girls and took them back to America.

—JAN STEPHENSON
**LPGA PROFESSIONAL AND
NATIVE OF AUSTRALIA IN 1991**

When Jack Nicklaus told me I was playing Seve Ballesteros, I took so many pills that I'm glad they don't have drug tests for golfers.

—FUZZY ZOELLER

ON HIS 1983 RYDER CUP MATCH, WHICH HE HALVED

You don't expect to be hit by a small white ball while walking through a meadow in Russia.

—PROFESSOR ALEXY NIKOLOV
BEFORE PERESTROIKA,
NOTING THAT FEWER THAN 300
RUSSIANS PLAY GOLF

Did you know? You have to demonstrate a minimum competence just to get on the course. You need a "green card."

—SWEDEN'S JESPER PARNEVIK
1994 BRITISH OPEN RUNNERUP,
DESCRIBING THE PROTOCOL
OF SWEDISH GOLF

ON
FANS AND
THE MEDIA

That wee body in the red jack canna play gouf.

—A SPECTATOR, COMMENTING ON ALLAN ROBERTSON'S POOR PLAY IN A MATCH WHERE HE WAS PARTNERED WITH TOM MORRIS AGAINST THE DUNN BROTHERS IN 1849. ROBERTSON, THE FIRST NOTEWORTHY GOLF PROFESSIONAL, WAS THE LEADING PLAYER OF HIS ERA.

The sonofabitch went in!

—JIMMY DEMARET
DESCRIBING LEW WORSHAM'S
140-YARD EAGLE APPROACH SHOT
ON THE FINAL HOLE THAT
WON HIM THE 1953 WORLD
CHAMPIONSHIP OF GOLF

Hagen was at home with all classes of society, far more than Dempsey or Ruth, the other great champions of the twenties, whom he resembled in the blackness of his hair, his amazing magnetism, his love of admiring crowds, and his rise from humble beginnings.

—GENE SARAZEN
IN HIS BOOK *THIRTY YEARS OF CHAMPIONSHIP GOLF*

The gallery becomes almost a part of the course and part of the round, to the experienced competitor, either he can play with a gallery following him or he can't—and if he can't, of course, the gallery doesn't follow him.

—BOBBY JONES

I would have worried if he didn't want
a photograph.

—BABE ZAHARIAS
**REGARDING AN OVERZEALOUS
PHOTOGRAPHER AT THE
BRITISH LADIES' CHAMPIONSHIP**

I am staying in the house
on Tobacco Road that Jeeter
Lester moved out of.

—SPORTS WRITER JIM MURRAY
APPRAISING HIS
ACCOMMODATIONS WHILE
COVERING THE MASTERS
IN THE OLD DAYS

I'm sitting there with the press, all pleased and comfortable, and when Arnie holes the thirty-footer they leave me like I got the pox.

—KEN VENTURI
AFTER PALMER DROPPED
A 30-FOOT BIRDIE PUTT
ON THE FINAL HOLE
TO WIN THE 1960 MASTERS,
WHICH VENTURI THOUGHT
HE HAD WON

Golfers cannot do their best playing to empty fairways any better than actors can give a fine performance to empty chairs.

—BOB HARLOW

**THE PGA'S FIRST FULL-TIME
TOUR DIRECTOR, IN 1929**

I wouldn't be here if there wasn't a golf tournament here. They're all the same—greens, tees. I'm here because there's money to be won.

—LEE TREVINO
WHEN ASKED BY A GALLERY
MEMBER WHETHER HE LIKED
THE PINEHURST NO. 2 COURSE,
SITE OF THE 1994 SENIOR OPEN

Most difficult of all is trying to be "a good sport." You are compelled to do many things you don't give two hoots about. To go on parties when you just long to be in bed, to be nice to all sorts of people, ask all sorts of favors.

—GLENNA COLLET VARE

Please give me the chance I've
been fighting for all week.

—HAROLD "JUG" MCSPADEN
TO PHOTOGRAPHERS WHO BROKE
HIS CONCENTRATION ON THE LAST
HOLE OF REGULATION MATCH PLAY
IN THE FINAL OF THE 1937 PGA
CHAMPIONSHIP. HE MISSED A
FOUR-FOOT PUTT FOR THE WIN
THEN LOST TO DENNY SHUTE ON
THE FIRST PLAYOFF HOLE.

At least I'm going to get a chance to meet her.

—A FAN WHO, IN 1978, WAS
BLOODIED WHEN HIT
BY AN ERRANT SHOT
BY NANCY LOPEZ, THEN
IN HER FIRST FULL YEAR
ON THE LPGA TOUR

I just love to see you guys with long hair, because you can't see. I never saw a hippie playing golf.

—BERT YANCEY

**PGA PRO AND FORMER
WEST POINT CADET, ADDRESSING
THE PRESS IN THE 1970S**

You know I thought our English football (soccer) crowds were bad, but this is worse.

—IAN WOOSNAM

TO PETER JACOBSEN AFTER
HEARING OBSCENITIES FROM THE
U.S. OPEN GALLERY AT MEDINAH
BECAUSE JACOBSEN WAS A
KNOWN PORTLAND TRAILBLAZER
FAN AND THE MIDWESTERN
CROWD FAVORED THE BULLS

I think you all know pretty well how much I feel. I suppose the sun got me a little. I got a little tired, I guess I got a little emotional coming up 18.

—ARNOLD PALMER

AGE 64, AT A PRESS CONFERENCE AFTER HIS FINAL U.S. OPEN AT OAKMONT IN 1994

I really like the attention. I guess I'm sort of a ham.

—LPGA PROFESSIONAL,
6' 2" CAROL MANN,
COMMENTING ON HER HEIGHT AND
THE ATTENTION IT BRINGS HER

If she's dumb enough to play, I'm dumb enough to let her.

—MRS. TILLIE STACEY
MOTHER OF HOLLIS STACEY,
THEN THE DEFENDING GIRLS
JUNIOR CHAMPION (1971),
WHEN HOLLIS PLAYED WITH
TENDONITIS IN HER RIGHT WRIST

Whip the gringo!

—LEE TREVINO'S FANS, URGING HIM
ON DURING HIS SUCCESSFUL RUN
AT THE 1968 U.S. OPEN AT OAK HILL

You figured out who you thought you could beat and you challenged him. And you hoped you didn't get Leondard Dodson because he'd pay a guy to follow you around with a camera and click it on your backswing.

—JIMMY DEMARET

DESCRIBING HOW PAIRINGS WERE ARRIVED AT DURING THE SAN FRANCISCO MATCH PLAY CHAMPIONSHIP IN THE 1930S

Right here Jack.

—SIGNS HELD UP BY ARNIE'S ARMY
BEHIND WATER HAZARDS
AND BUNKERS AT THE 1967
U.S. OPEN AT BALTUSROL

The 1922 U.S. Open was the first USGA event with an admission fee for spectators. In less than four years, thanks to the popularity of Bobby Jones and other players, those fees became the organization's chief source of income.

—*GOLF MAGAZINE*, DECEMBER 1994

I don't think we've ever achieved in golf television—and this may be presumptuous of me—the right balance between audio and video. The developments in the video have been just sensational, and a lot of that was pioneered by ABC. But the audio doesn't match that, mostly because they (announcers) talk too much.

—SANDY TATUM
OF THE USGA

Woods makes people awestruck, Mickelson gives them the feeling he cares. Fans respect Woods. They love Mickelson.

—**JEFF RUDE,** DESCRIBING THE DIFFERENCE BETWEEN TIGER WOODS AND PHIL MICKELSON IN *GOLFWEEK*

ON
ENDINGS

If they don't have golf in heaven
then I'm not going.

—AN INSCRIPTION ON A PILLOW
IN ARNOLD PALMER'S HOME

His biggest game is over.
He putted out.

—PASTOR EDWIN A. SHROEDER

AT WALTER HAGEN'S FUNERAL

IN OCTOBER OF 1969

I'm just tired. It has been a long grind. There were days when I thought I would scream if I had to go to the course. It was week-in week-out for years. I tried to give my best to golf. Now I want to realize a dream. I've got my dad and mother with me and . . . Well, that's the story.

—BYRON NELSON
RETIRING FROM THE
PROFESSIONAL TOUR IN 1946
AT AGE 34

And softly by the nineteenth hole
   reclined

Make game of that which maketh game
   of thee

—ROBERT K. RISK
**IN "THE GOLFAIYET OF
DUFOR HY-YAM" (1919)**

Try to feel that you are looser and more decisive on the eighteenth hole than you were on the first. Fell more likely to coin the last tournament of the season than the first.

—DR. BOB ROTELLA
SPORTS PSYCHOLOGIST

Don't ever get old.

—BEN HOGAN

**IN 1971, WHEN HE HAD TO
WITHDRAW FROM
THE HOUSTON OPEN
AFTER 11 HOLES DUE TO
PAIN AND FATIGUE**

I don't want to be eulogized
until I'm dead.

—BEN HOGAN

**DECLINING AN INVITATION TO BE
THE HONOREE AT JACK NICKLAUS'
MEMORIAL TOURNAMENT**

My frustration centers on not being able to play as well as I once did. I still could play regularly, but don't want to. I was out there from 1955 through 1969. That's fifteen years of motels and competitive pressure. Now I play only a handful of events. I've played six tournaments this year. Last year I played only two.

—MICKEY WRIGHT
IN A *GOLF DIGEST* INTERVIEW
IN 1976

I never heard a word said against him
except a solitary complaint that, in the
lightness of his heart, he played pi-
brochs (musical pieces on a bagpipe)
round the drowsy town at
the midnight hour. What would we not
give to hear those pipes again.

—ANDREW LANG

**REMEMBERING SCOTTISH GOLFER
F. M. TAIT, BRITISH AMATEUR
CHAMPION (1896, 1898) AND
BRITISH OPEN CHAMPION
(1896, 1897), WHO DIED AT
AGE 30 IN THE BOER WAR**

I'm going to die in a tournament on the golf course. They'll just throw me in a bunker and build it up a little bit.

—LEE TREVINO
WINNER OF FIVE VARDON
TROPHIES FOR LOW SCORING
AVERAGE ON THE PGA TOUR

People have always said,
"Jack, I wish I could play like
you." Well now they can.

—JACK NICKLAUS
IN 1994 AT AGE 54 AND
STRUGGLING WITH HIS GAME

I don't want to get old, but I don't have much choice, so if it will help my golf like these guys, then it won't be so bad.

—JOSE MARIA OLAZABAL
AFTER LOSING TO GREG NORMAN AND NICK PRICE IN THE 1994 GRAND SLAM OF GOLF

I'm old enough to be most of their fathers. They don't know whether to call me Mr. Sigel or to call me Jay.

—JAY SIGEL

AGE 49, PLAYING IN HIS 27TH CONSECUTIVE U.S. AMATEUR IN 1993 AGAINST A FIELD DOMINATED BY COLLEGE-AGE PLAYERS

The road's getting shorter and narrower, but I'll play wherever the pigeons land.

—SAM SNEAD

AT 81 YEARS OLD IN EARLY 1994

Life is a journey and it must be enjoyed—
and, like golf, part of the fun is that you
never know where it might take you.

—DR. BOB ROTELLA
SPORTS PSYCHOLOGIST

When you die, what you take with you is what you leave behind. If you don't share, no matter how much you have, you will always be poor.

—CHI-CHI RODRIGUEZ
WINNER OF MANY AWARDS FOR HIS COMMUNITY SERVICE TO JUNIOR GOLFERS AND OTHERS

Captain in 1865, Sir John (Low) played well into his 90s, and took to his pony when walking became difficult during the latter part of the round, dismounting between shots.

—RICHARD MACKENZIE
IN HIS BOOK *A WEE NIP AT THE 19TH HOLE* **(1991)**

Julius Boros died on a golf course one quiet May afternoon and took the swing of our dreams with him. . . . No one ever swung a club with such nonchalance as Boros. He had, more than any other player of his time, the game's most exclusive quality: effortless power. And it came to him as naturally as taking a drag on a cigarette.

—JERRY TARDE
EDITOR OF *GOLF DIGEST* IN 1994

Show respect to Sarah

You golfers passing by;

She's the only person on this course,

Who can't improve her lie.

—RHYME RESULTING FROM A GOLF
COURSE BEING BUILT AROUND
THE GRAVE OF SARAH WALLACE
(D. 1862) AT SHORE ACRES

Deeply regretted by numerous friends and all golfers, he thrice in succession won the championship belt and held it without rivalry and yet without envy, his many amiable qualities being no less acknowledged than his golfing achievements.

—THE INSCRIPTION ON THE GRAVE
OF YOUNG TOM MORRIS,
WINNER OF FOUR BRITISH OPENS,
AND THE DOMINANT PLAYER
OF HIS ERA, IN ST. ANDREWS

INDEX